The SEER DIMENSIONS

ACTIVATING
YOUR PROPHETIC SIGHT
TO SEE THE UNSEEN

JENNIFER LECLAIRE

DESTINY IMAGE® PUBLISHERS, INC.
P.O. Box 310, Shippensburg, PA 17257-0310
"Promoting Inspired Lives."

Cover design by Eileen Rockwell
Interior design by Terry Clifton

This book and all other Destiny Image and Destiny Image Fiction books are available at Christian bookstores and distributors worldwide.

For more information on foreign distributors, call 717-532-3040.

Or reach us on the Internet: www.destinyimage.com

ISBN 13 TP: 978-0-7684-5386-7
ISBN 13 EBook: 978-0-7684-5387-4
HC ISBN: 978-0-7684-5388-1
LP ISBN: 978-0-7684-5389-8

For Worldwide Distribution, Printed in the U.S.A.
1 2 3 4 5 6 7 8 / 23 22 21 20 19

DEDICATION

I dedicate this book the pioneers in the seer realms, many of whom were misunderstood, persecuted, and rejected by the Body of Christ. Many have gone on to glory and may never read these words, but this new generation of seers would not rise without the foundation you laid. I, at the same time, dedicate this book to the new generation of seers who are hungry for the Lord and looking for answers to real questions in their hearts.

ACKNOWLEDGMENTS

I am grateful for seers around me like Vanessa Angelini, Emma Stark and Benjamin Sleep who sharpen me and encourage me in the journey. I also want to acknowledge Larry Sparks and the team at Destiny Image for being a prophetic voice in the Christian publishing world. Thanks for believing in this book!

FOREWORD

by James W Goll

What an honor to be composing the foreword for a book called *The Seer Dimensions*. As one of the fathers today in the global prayer and prophetic movements, growing in the understanding and instruction of this seer dimension, is both highly personal and highly significant. In fact, it is imperative that the global prophetic movement embraces the gift and the impact of The Seer Dimensions. More has been known, taught, demonstrated and empowered in the smooth flowing naba dimension of the prophetic. Oh how refreshing it is to bubble up and gush forth like a fountain!

But there are those, who are also prophetically called and gifted and they are more visual by gift and calling. These anointed vessels have historically have been referred to as seers. When my book, *The Seer*, came out, is became a modern day pioneer work for the body of Christ at large. I had no idea the depth and width of impact that book would have. It gave language and biblical grounding for an entire emerging generation of seer-prophets. Over the years, as more authentic gifted ones have come forth, understanding and experience has both increased.

I highly value those who move in the gifts of the Spirit, but also those who equip others to operate in what God has freely given to them. That is the key to multiplication. This is one of the primary reasons I rejoice over the content of this book, *The Seer Dimensions*. It picks up the narrative that I helped develop and brings us additional teaching tools filled with progressive revelation and understanding for our times.

We are truly living in the Convergence of the Ages! If Jesus is saving some of the best till last, then the contents of this book might just qualify as some of that. This is one of the best books I have ever read on the dimensions of the seer!

With Gratitude,

Dr. James W Goll
Founder of God Encounters Ministries
Author, Communications Trainer and Recording Artist

CONTENTS

INTRODUCTION

The seer realm is nothing new. Adam was the first seer in the Bible. He saw in the spirit without restriction because he was without sin. After the fall, the enemy put blinders on our eyes (see John 12:40). Christ came to take the blinders off, but the seer gift has not yet been fully restored to the Body of Christ. In this hour, God is opening the eyes of seers and seeing people all over the world.

If you are reading this book, He has either opened your eyes or you are curious about the seer realm. That's a good thing. I started out in the realm of the prophetic in the *nabi*, or auditory realm. My spiritual curiosity, combined with faith, opened my eyes wider and wider until I started seeing frequently, in great detail and with accuracy in the spirit.

In any discussion of the spirit realms, we have to have faith. That Scripture, *"We walk by faith and not by sight"* is not meant to negate our spiritual vision (2 Cor. 5:7 DRA). By contrast, our spiritual vision works by faith just like our spiritual hearing works by faith. Faith is the master key to seeing in the spirit.

Right now choose to believe the world you came from is much more vibrant than the world you are currently living in. By force of your will choose to maintain that belief even in the face of warfare, doubt, unbelief, and criticism until it renews your mind. Faith is nothing if it is not tested. It can be fleeting, or it can be for perpetuity. It all depends on you and how strong your belief is, and you will need to remember this as you read through the pages of this book.

With still only a relative few books on the seer realm on the market—some controversial—awakened believers who are pressing in to what God is showing them can't always find trusted resources that combine scriptural truths with experiential realities.

I hope this book opens your eyes. If your eyes are already open, we pray God opens them wider and helps you navigate, with integrity and faith, the seer realms.

CHAPTER 1

CALLING ALL SEERS

I once believed intercessors were the most misunderstood operatives in the Body of Christ. Many pastors still don't appreciate their contribution to the local church—and prayer is relegated to the back of the house. Many believers have labeled intercessors weird, odd, strange, or out there. Although I've seen a greater appreciation for this office in recent years, intercessors—those who carry prayer burdens, enter deep travail, and tend to isolate themselves for hours on end to stand in the gap—are still widely misunderstood.

Likewise, the church has not always been kind to its prophets. As I wrote in my first-ever book, *The Heart of the Prophetic*, prophets have a history of getting beaten, imprisoned, and even sawed in half by those who call themselves godly (a.k.a. the religious church). Prophets have been misunderstood, and many denominations in the Body of Christ still widely rejected them, despite the work of my spiritual father, Bishop Bill Hamon, and many others who helped restore this office beginning in the 1980s.

Throughout church history, seers have been at times revered for their gift and at times persecuted. Despite the reality of seers in the Bible, the Body of Christ has been more accepting of dreams as common to man but has been less accepting seeing in the spirit realm through visions, trances, and heavenly encounters. In fact, many who operate in these realms have been labeled heretics. Of course, seers have existed since creation. God created us in His image (see Gen. 1:27). He is the ultimate seer. Now, God is emphasizing seers at a level the modern church has never witnessed before.

Consider this: although God used the word *prophet* to refer to Abraham in the Book of Genesis, the word *seer* was the more common name for a prophet up until Samuel's day (see 1 Sam. 9:9). Despite the biblical use of the term and examples in Scripture, seers have been the lesser known agents in the prophetic realm—until now. God is shining a spotlight on seers and is opening the eyes of more believers to see in the same way He shined a light on prophets in the 1980s and opened the ears of believers to hear and say.

In the New Testament the Holy Spirit continued emphasizing the word *prophet*, and when the office of the prophet was restored, we largely focused on the auditory ability of this gift rather than the seer flow. I believe that was God's intention because hearing prophets could have received instruction to press into the seer realm but, at large, the movement remained about "the word of the Lord came unto me saying." Millions of people around the world began to receive prophetic words. Believers were activated in the simple gift of prophecy, and they began to speak words of edification, exhortation, and comfort, according to 1 Corinthians 14:3.

Put another way, we have largely neglected the seer realms as the Church of Jesus Christ. We have relegated seers to the fringes of the prophetic, partially through rejection of those who operate in the gift and partly out of ignorance, and perhaps partly because of the perfect timing of the Lord to bring seers to the fore. Now that Jesus is emphasizing the seer realm of the prophetic, it's time to embrace this gift and learn to navigate it.

What Exactly Is a Seer?

Let's back up for a minute and answer this question: What is a seer? *Merriam-Webster's* dictionary defines *seer* as "one that sees; one that predicts events or developments; a person credited with extraordinary moral and spiritual insight."[1] In short, seers are prophets who receive their revelation by peering through the veil of the spirit realm as God allows. Not all prophets are seers, but all seers are prophets. The seer is a type of prophet. Most prophets can see, and most seers can hear. These are two streams from the same Holy Ghost river.

Prophets as we've come to know them in the modern-day prophetic movement operate in the *naba* realm. *Naba* is a Hebrew word that means "to prophesy, speak as a prophet; prophecy has its focus on encouraging or restoring covenant faithfulness, the telling of future events encourages obedience or warns against disobedience."[2]

Again, not all prophets are seers, but all seers are prophets. At first glance, some may ask, "What does it really matter if they are all prophets?" God distinguished them in His Word, so it matters. Giving a natural analogy, when you go to the hospital, there are many kinds of doctors. They are all trained in practicing medicine, but they specialize in different areas. Some are cardiovascular specialists. Some are ear, nose, and throat specialists. Some are orthopedic specialists. I don't want to go to a foot doctor to have heart surgery or a heart doctor for an eye exam.

Prophets and seers are two streams of the prophetic anointing, but they specialize in different aspects of the anointing. Even within the realm of prophet and seer there are many different distinctions and types of prophetic flows.

Seers consistently have dreams or visions, see angels or demons, see words written over people's heads. Seers see lights and colors. Seers may see Jesus or heaven or hell. A seer perceives with spiritual eyes—the eyes of the Holy Spirit. Indeed, seers perceive, detect, experience, visualize, recognize, become aware, encounter, examine, watch, explore, judge, encounter, discern, look, investigate, inquire, receive, and apprehend— and equip, according to the Ephesians 4:11 fivefold ascension gift mandate.

Biblically speaking, there are several Hebrew words for *see* that we need to understand. One Hebrew word for *seer* is *ra'ah*, which means, "to see, look, view; to realize, know, consider; to be selected; to become visible, appear, show oneself; to be seen; to cause to see, show; to be shown; to look at each other, meet with; a general word for visual perception."[3] The Hebrew word *ro'eh* means "a seer, vision."[4]

Then there's the Hebrew word *chozeh*, which means, "seer, one who receives a communication from God, with a possible focus that the message had a visual component; agreement."[5] And *chazah* means "to see, to look, observe, gaze, by extension: to choose (one thing or another); to have visions, to prophesy."[6]

Seers have been around since the beginning—Adam could see in the spirit. The enemy has worked to hide this gift from the Body of Christ. The spirit of Delilah has worked to blind the eyes of the seers through temptation. The spirit of religion wants to keep seers in a dark cave of rejection. But God is once again emphasizing this gift, which I believe will be vital in the end-times. Before we move on to where we're going, though, it's important to see how God has restored the seer prophet over the twentieth and twenty-first centuries little by little.

William Branham and the History of Modern-Day Seers

We remember the late William Branham's ability to see in the spirit. Branham rose to fame during the Voice of Healing movement and was known for healing manifestations with the help of an angel. He once spoke of vision of a little boy being raised from the dead. Two years later he came upon the scene of this horrific sight in the earth realm.

"I seen a little boy being raised from the dead," Branham said. "I went down in Miami and there predicted it before thousands of people."[7]

Branham not only predicted it, he described with minute detail what the young boy would look like, right down to his hair style and his eye color. Then it happened. Two years later, Branham was in Finland when he came upon the scene a deadly car crash. An American-made car struck and killed two children.[8]

As Branham tells it, the car knocked one of the children into a tree and crushed his brains. The car rolled over the other child and he was lying dead underneath some coats Branham says his companions went over to look at the little boy and came back crying. They tried to convince Branham to go see for himself, but he declined because he had a son nearly the same age.[9]

"Finally, they persuaded me to go over and when I went to look at the little lad, I looked down at him and my heart was breaking to see the little fella and I turned away," Branham said. "And when I turned away, something laid its hand on my shoulder. I thought it was Brother [G. Gordon] Lindsay and I looked around and there was nobody around me at all and the hand was still on my shoulder. See how stupid a preacher can be?"[10]

Branham recalls that the boy's parents were on their way to the sad scene. The child had been dead about thirty minutes. Branham said he looked down twice and then asked someone to raise the coat off the boy's lifeless body. At that moment, the Lord replayed in his mind the vision he had seen in Georgia of a little boy being raised from the dead. It was the same boy lying on the ground![11]

"Every bone in his body was broken and his foot run through his sock. It was that boy perfectly....Oh my, what a feeling. You could take every scientist in the world and stand them there and every demon out of torment could be standing there—it's going to happen anyhow.... God's already said it and it's going to be done," Branham said. "I said, 'If that boy isn't on his feet in the next five minutes I'm a false prophet.'"[12]

As the story goes, Branham knelt down over the boy just as he had seen himself do in the vision and prayed, "Lord, God of heavens and earth, over in the homeland you showed me this vision while passing through Georgia one night....I pray to thee Lord God that now that you will confirm the word so they might know that you're still the Lord Jesus and that Finland would know that You are the resurrection from the dead."[13]

With that, Branham laid his hands on the lifeless boy and called for the spirit of death to give the boy back. Immediately, he said, the little boy jumped up screaming and running around. He was raised from the dead and his broken bones healed—all in an instant. The news spread all over Finland. The mayor certified the event, and it goes down in church history as one of the most astounding miracles ever. Branham waged prophetic warfare against death based on a vision from the Lord and God was glorified.[14]

Paul Cain Picks Up the Seer Baton

Paul Cain served William Branham, who commissioned him when he was just seventeen years old. Although Cain had controversies while he lived, his ministry endured seventy-six years before he passed away in 2019. Like Billy Graham, Oral Roberts, and Jack Coe, Cain had a tent ministry that saw tens of thousands of people gather. But Cain was more than a healing evangelist. He was a seer of seers. He had a recurring vision of stadiums filled to overflowing with people seeking a touch from God and finding salvation in Him.

> "Paul also served as a consultant to Central Intelligence Agency—Paranormal Division, a consultant to the FBI, and was a presidential consultant and special envoy for three presidents," says Jeff Jansen, senior leader of Global

Fire Church and founder of Global Fire Ministries International. "Paul ministered to many national and international leaders and during the Clinton Administration, Paul went to Iraq to meet with Saddam Hussein. He also met with many spiritual key church and denominational leaders."[15]

A member of the controversial Kansas City Prophets, Cain, who also encouraged Mike Bickle during the early years of the International House of Prayer, is perhaps best remembered for his stadium Christianity vision released twenty years before his passing and less than two years before Lou Engle launched TheCall to start filing stadiums with young people to pray, fast, and worship. It's worth reading this significant prophecy in full:

> What if God poured out of Heaven some kind of a great outpouring and His sovereignty and righteousness and justice and love and His eternal life and omniscience and omnipotence and omnipresent and immutability and veracity just dumped all over you.
>
> Azusa Street was instituted, and people went there, and they beheld the baptizer and became the baptized. Then they beheld the healer and became the healed and then all of a sudden God has saved the best for the last. The Jesus People came in because they beheld the Savior and became the saved. Look out California. There's something greater than a tidal wave. There's something greater than a gigantic cataclysmic earthquake coming. God will shake the Earth once more and His glory is about to revealed in His people. Sons and daughters of God are going to be introduced in this meeting. Something's going to come so strong to you that you won't even know that there had been any baptism of

the Holy Ghost compared to the enormous baptism you're about to receive.

I tell you, that cloud is coming. That cloud is coming. For they will be the faceless generation of men who will stand on a platform with thousands and multitudes and masses all about. And the news media—ABC, NBC, CBS, CNN—will be saved.

"Ladies and gentlemen, we have no news tonight to report, but good news. The whole world is going mad over Jesus. They're falling on their face and saying, 'Jesus is Lord of all—of all! There's no sports news tonight because all the football stadiums and all the ballparks and all the colosseums are filled to overflowing with thousands gathering." They're saying, "We have a resurrection over here." And then twisted mangled bodies are being made straight. And then the news announcers are saying, "Ladies and gentlemen, we don't know who these people are. They're almost faceless, and they're speaking great wisdom and they're speaking things that are bringing about resurrections and bringing about healings."

And I want you to know it will happen, my friends, and the church of the Lord Jesus Christ will once again become the first line of defense. She'll be the only cure for AIDS. She'll be the only cure for communicable diseases that medical science will never be able to heal.[16]

Intercessors around the world are praying into this prophecy, waiting for the full manifestation of what Cain saw.

Bob Jones Brings Language to Seer Movement

A contemporary of Paul Cain who passed away in 2014, Bob Jones was also part of the Kanas City Prophets. This seer had astounding visions and heavenly encounters, but also helped give important language to the seer realm. When asked, what is a seer, Jones replied, "A seer is everything. Prophets are the eyes, but seers are the entire head: eyes, smell, taste and feelings. That is what Isaiah 29:10 says: *He has shut your eyes, the prophets; And He has covered your heads, the seers.*"[17]

With this, he gave the loaf of bread example that helped distinguish the seer from the *nabi* prophet. When your eyes are open, you can see the loaf of bread, but when your eyes are closed you cannot, even though you may know it's there.

"As a seer, you can move in all five realms, and because of that, you are more discerning. The enemy is never able to fully shut you down," Jones said. "The prophet can be momentarily blinded, but if the enemy blinds you, you will still be able to hear, smell, taste, and feel. If the enemy comes against your feelings, you'll still be able to see, hear, smell, and taste. A seer prophecies by all five senses, and so the seers move in stronger discernment."[18]

This is indeed one of the key differences between the *nabi* and the *chozeh*. Jones explains it this way:

> The prophet can speak the future, but the seer can see what the people need to let go of in the past, tell them what the Lord is saying to them today, and declare what the Lord is offering them tomorrow. You can go right into their minds and see where the pain is coming from and what is still affecting and controlling their lives. Seers can help people forgive—usually themselves, help clean their minds out, and invite the Lord there.
>
> Seers can knock on a person's front door, come in, and visit with that person without saying a word. A prophet can only prophecy as the faith arises. A lot of times, a prophet is just a person who really comes forth in faith, and that

faith activates him so he can speak clearly. That is what Nathan the prophet was. He prophecies by the faith that rose in him. But a seer can have all five senses.

A seer can feel the strongholds of a town. If you enter a town and feel lust, lust owns that town. If you feel depression, it's a depressed place. As you come in there, you'll take on the feelings of that town, country, or person, whether they are good or bad. You'll know where there is self-rejection, because of what you feel. If you're ministering to somebody who has self-rejection, you'll feel it coming at yourself, and you must never take any of these things personally.

And so, with Jones we saw the beginning of education of the seer gift, just as with Hamon we saw a movement to educate the Body of Christ on the office of the prophet.

John Paul Jackson Opens the Dream World

Another late seer, John Paul Jackson, founder of Streams Ministries International, opened up the dream realm for the average believer and brought language to dream interpreters. He operated heavily in dreams and visions—including the well-known The Coming Perfect Storm—and, until his untimely passing in 2015, ministered to the masses prophetically.

Perhaps more importantly, he awakened dreams and visions in the body, and equipped us to interpret them rightly. He even hosted a show on Daystar Television called *Dreams & Mysteries with John Paul Jackson* and interpreted tens of thousands of dreams. He explained:

> Dreams are one of mankind's greatest mysteries. Dreams use a symbolic language. To have a correct interpretation one has to know the dream source and dream code. Imagine if the dream you had last night contained the answer

that you had been looking for, and you didn't know it? Knowing the meaning of a dream can be life changing.[19]

With words like these and clear teaching that came from the authority of one who walked in this realm, Jackson is still inspiring current and will inspire future generations of people to pursue the meanings of their dreams. He truly fulfilled the Ephesians 4 mandate to equip believers.

Kim Clement's Dramatic Visions

Kim Clement, the South African seer-prophet-worship leader who passed into glory in 2016 at the age of sixty, experienced dramatic visions and released prophetic words that are still coming to pass in our day. One of the most interesting examples is how Clement prophesied the election of President Donald Trump—"Trump shall become a trumpet."[20] Trump, as we know, did become president after Clement's passing. But Clement's ministry was also marked by dreams and visions.

He once told TBN, "I knew I was a prophet when I had certain kinds of dreams about the future and when I spoke about people actually hated me for it....I would see futuristic things and it would cause so much stirring." Indeed, Clement had dramatic visions and inspired even naba prophets to press into the vision realm with words like these:

> Prophets today are inspirational and they're all about vision; they're all about sight. That's what prophets are called to do. A prophet is one that is demanded by God to see. He has to have vision. He has to have vision beyond this time so that he can bring it to the people. You know, in Hosea chapter 12, Hosea speaks about prophets and he says, God says, "I've also spoken by the prophets and I have multiplied visions."

Clement's prophetic words and visions continue coming to pass after his untimely death, inspiring more prophets to speak forth what they see. On May 18, 2013, Clement had what he called a "very, very clear vision" about the year 2018. The man of God was seeing five years into the future a significant historical event that few at the time likely believe:

The Lord said to me that on the eighteenth day of May, 2018, Israel is going to experience something of a great freedom and peace for a while and that we are to be there in May on the eighteenth. I didn't realize then at the time that when I was praying this that it was actually the seventieth anniversary. I may have known it, but I didn't think about it when the Lord spoke to me yesterday. It was clear that He said we must do a massive gathering in 2018. And then He said something. He said China will even fight for Israel, fight for them. I don't know if this is a war or what it is, but He said they must be very careful. So I'm saying that all now because I think that's in the future, quite a bit in the future, some of the stuff I got in China but only got clarity on it…now when I reached the garden.[21]

James Goll Connects Seers and Intercession

James Goll also helped give language to the seer realm, but he brought intercession and the prophetic together in a profound way. In fact, he is the father of the modern-day prophetic intercession movement. Goll, founder of God Encounters Ministries, has a heart that beats for intercession.

Goll wrote one of the first credible books on the seer realm, aptly called *The Seer: The Power of Visions, Dreams, and Open Heavens*. For millions of Christians he has answered questions such as: How does visionary revelation happen? Can it be trusted? Where does it fit into your life and today's church? Can any believer become a seer? Is it a prophetic dimension reserved for the spiritually gifted?

Ultimately, Goll helped awakening seers and seeing people with statements like this from his book:

> As Christians, we are called to be a people of vision. We must learn to set a goal or target in front of our eyes to gaze upon. It is only when we aim at something that we have any chance of hitting it!
>
> The apostle Paul set his sights on knowing Christ, which he acknowledged was a lifelong process:
>
> *Brethren, I do not regard myself as having laid hold of it yet; but one thing I do: forgetting what lies behind and reaching forward to what lies ahead, I press on toward the goal for the prize of the upward call of God in Christ Jesus. Let us therefore, as many as are perfect, have this attitude* (Phil. 3:13–15a [NASB]).
>
> Like Paul, we need to be a people of vision. Let us set our sights on the Lord and aim at His goals.[22]

Seers and Seeing People Rising

Following the Charismatic movement in the 1960s that emphasized spiritual gifts, God began to restore the office of the prophet in the 1980s, but there was strong emphasis on the *naba* prophets, those who experienced "the word of the Lord came to me saying" aspect of the prophetic. Although some seers rose up during that time, the emphasis was on prophets and prophetic people. Impartation and activation made up the thrust in the Body of Christ.

If you look around, you will surely notice times are changing in the Body of Christ—and this book is proof. God is raising up companies of seers and congregations of seeing people who prophesy both by faith and by sight—spiritual sight. And like their fivefold prophet counterparts, seers also have an Ephesians 4:11 equipping mandate. The Lord put this mandate on me heavily in November 2017.

On the last day of the Global Prophets Summit with Cindy Jacobs, James Goll, Stacey Campbell, and others, I was teaching about the seer's anointing on Facebook Live from my hotel room. I had no idea the Lord was going to overwhelm me with His presence. (You can still find the video on YouTube.) During the broadcast, I began to feel a mantle fall upon my shoulders. At first, I didn't know what exactly was happening. I ended the broadcast and the anointing remained. It was a profound experience, similar to how the Lord has mantled me in the past.

I asked the Lord what it meant, and He explained He was giving me a new anointing, commissioning. and mandate to raise up seers and seeing people. He instructed me to launch a School of Seers and a Company of Seers, which I did as fast as I could. Since then, He has given me more and more revelation and practical insights to help seers understand their gift and believers break through obstacles to seeing in the spirit. Some, but not all, of those insights are found in the pages of this book.

Is God calling you to walk in this realm? That's likely the reason you picked up this book. Pray this prayer now: "Father, give me a hunger to learn and grow in the seer realm. Help me understand and navigate the seer realms. Teach me to walk in this gift for Your glory, in Jesus' name. Amen."

Chapter 2

Everyone Can See in the Spirit

E veryone has the God-given ability in the spirit. That's right, everyone. You don't have to be a prophet to prophesy, and you don't have to be a seer to see in the spirit. Consider the simple gift of prophecy. Outlined in 1 Corinthians 12 among the other eight gifts of the Holy Spirit, the simple gift of prophecy is available to all believers. Anybody can prophesy.

The enemy has tried to keep most believers ignorant about their ability to move in spiritual gifts, especially prophecy and especially the seer realm. Paul worked even in the early church to overcome such ignorance. By the inspiration of the Holy Spirit, Paul wrote in 1 Corinthians 12:1–11:

> *Now concerning spiritual gifts, brethren, I do not want you to be ignorant: You know that you were Gentiles, carried away to these dumb idols, however you were led. Therefore I make known to you that no one speaking by the Spirit of God calls Jesus accursed, and no one can say that Jesus is Lord except by the Holy Spirit.*

There are diversities of gifts, but the same Spirit. There are differences of ministries, but the same Lord. And there are diversities of activities, but it is the same God who works all in all. But the manifestation of the Spirit is given to each one for the profit of all: for to one is given the word of wisdom through the Spirit, to another the word of knowledge through the same Spirit, to another faith by the same Spirit, to another gifts of healings by the same Spirit, to another the working of miracles, to another prophecy, to another discerning of spirits, to another different kinds of tongues, to another the interpretation of tongues. But one and the same Spirit works all these things, distributing to each one individually as He wills.

Now you are officially informed. The Holy Spirit distributes gifts individually as He wills. We are called to *"pursue love, desire spiritual gifts, but especially that we may prophesy"* (1 Cor. 14:1). That word for *desire* is the Greek word *zeloo*, which means to "burn with zeal."[1] You should pursue God for the manifestation of spiritual gifts, especially prophecy, in your life.

You can relate that verse to seeing in the spirit. Prophecy includes the realms of hearing and seeing. Proverbs 20:12 speaks of *"the hearing ear and the seeing eye, the Lord has made them both."* The simple gift of prophecy is for edification, exhortation, and comfort. I submit to you that edification, exhortation, and comfort can come by way of what we hear or what we see. God wants us to be well-versed in His communication modes. If you can hear, you can see—or at least you have the capacity to see.

By contrast, just because you can prophesy doesn't mean you are a prophet—and just because you can see in the spirit doesn't make you a seer. But let me repeat that first statement again for emphasis: Everyone has the inherent ability to see in the spirit. You are included in that "everyone." Seers are prophets—a type of prophet—according to the Ephesians 4:11 paradigm. That means modern-day seers have a mandate to equip the saints for the work of the ministry—or put another way, to see in to the spirit at the level God opens to them.

The seer's Ephesians 4:11 mandate is the key thrust of this book. We are working to equip you to enter seer realms as the Holy Spirit leads. Whether you are a seer looking for language, Scripture, and understanding or a believer who wants to operate in seer realms, you'll find answers in this manuscript—answers that activate in you what God already gave you. First, we need to convince you that you can see in the spirit. It's likely you know you can or you would not have picked up this book, but let us give you scriptural proof to fuel your faith.

If a Donkey Can See...

Through the restoration of the prophetic movement, there's been a tongue-in-cheek saying that goes something like this: if God can speak through a donkey, He can speak through you. This relates back to Balaam, the prophet who King Balak wanted to hire to curse Israel. As you read this account, take notice of what it really says in Numbers 22:22–23:

> *Then God's anger was aroused because he went, and the Angel of the Lord took His stand in the way as an adversary against him. And he was riding on his donkey, and his two servants were with him. Now the donkey saw the Angel of the Lord standing in the way with His drawn sword in His hand, and the donkey turned aside out of the way and went into the field. So Balaam struck the donkey to turn her back onto the road.*

Let's stop right there. What happened? The donkey saw the angel. Ironically, the prophet could not see the angel—likely because he was in rebellion to the will of the Lord by agreeing to visit Balak. The donkey—God's creation—saw into the spirit realm what even the prophet missed. Don't you think if God can open the eyes of a donkey to the spirit world, He can open yours? Selah.

Let's continue with verses 24–27:

> *Then the Angel of the Lord stood in a narrow path between the vineyards, with a wall on this side and a wall on that side. And when the donkey saw the Angel of the Lord, she pushed herself against the wall and crushed Balaam's foot against the wall; so he struck her again. Then the Angel of the Lord went further, and stood in a narrow place where there was no way to turn either to the right hand or to the left. And when the donkey saw the Angel of the Lord, she lay down under Balaam; so Balaam's anger was aroused, and he struck the donkey with his staff.*

The donkey's eyes are wide open. The donkey saw and responded with greater faith and corresponding action to the unseen realm than the seen realm. This is our goal as seers and seeing people—to respond to what we clearly see with our spiritual eyes with as much or more faith and corresponding action as we see with our natural eyes. This is part of walking in the Spirit.

Again, you have this inherent ability as a born-again believer. If you can prophesy, you can see. As a matter of fact, even if you've never prophesied, you still have the ability to see. God wants your ears to see and your eyes to talk. In other words, He wants you fully activated.

But there's something else interesting in this passage, looking at verses 28–30:

> *Then the Lord opened the mouth of the donkey, and she said to Balaam, "What have I done to you, that you have struck me these three times?" And Balaam said to the donkey,*

"Because you have abused me. I wish there were a sword in my hand, for now I would kill you!" So the donkey said to Balaam, "Am I not your donkey on which you have ridden, ever since I became yours, to this day? Was I ever disposed to do this to you?" And he said, "No."

Notice this: the Lord opened the donkey's eyes before He opened the donkey's mouth. In reality, it's the same way in the Kingdom. God opens the eyes of our heart by way of conviction, then we open our mouths and confess our salvation. We become born-again with the ability to manifest the Kingdom according to the light that we have. We should pray then for more light and understanding that the entrance of God's Word brings (see Ps. 119:130).

That's not the end of the story. Read verses 31–33:

Then the Lord opened Balaam's eyes, and he saw the Angel of the Lord standing in the way with His drawn sword in His hand; and he bowed his head and fell flat on his face. And the Angel of the Lord said to him, "Why have you struck your donkey these three times? Behold, I have come out to stand against you, because your way is perverse before Me. The donkey saw Me and turned aside from Me these three times. If she had not turned aside from Me, surely I would also have killed you by now, and let her live."

Finally, we see Balaam's eyes opened. The donkey prophesied to the prophet, which got his attention. Then the preincarnate Christ opened his eyes and convicted him of his sin. How do we know that? Verse 34: *"And Balaam said to the Angel of the Lord, 'I have sinned, for I did not know You stood in the way against me. Now therefore, if it displeases You, I will turn back."*

So, then, if God can open a donkey's eyes, don't you think He can open your eyes? (The answer is yes.)

Equipped to See in the Last Days

The Bible makes many promises about the last days. Paul warned us, for example, that in the last days, perilous times will come (see 2 Tim. 3:1). In the last days, apostasy—turning away from the faith—will increase (see Matt. 24:12). In the last days, scoffers who walk according to their lusts will come (see 2 Pet. 3:3).

Indeed, there are a lot of sober prophecies in Scripture about the last days. However, there is an Old Testament prophecy that was re-prophesied in the New Testament, just after the outpouring of the Holy Spirit. This should encourage us and at the same time help us understand just how important the prophetic realm is in the last days.

That Old Testament prophecy came from the mouth of Joel: *"And it shall come to pass afterward that I will pour out My Spirit on all flesh; your sons and your daughters shall prophesy, your old men shall dream dreams, your young men shall see visions. And also on My menservants and on My maidservants I will pour out My Spirit in those days"* (Joel 2:28–29).

With Holy Spirit inspiration, Peter spoke forth this prophecy in Acts 2:17–18:

> *And it shall come to pass in the last days, says God, that I will pour out of My Spirit on all flesh; your sons and your daughters shall prophesy, your young men shall see visions, your old men shall dream dreams. And on My menservants and on My maidservants I will pour out My Spirit in those days; and they shall prophesy.*

Joel and Peter were both prophesying about the seer realm opening in conjunction with the outpouring—or baptism—of the Holy Spirit. In fact, Peter re-prophesied this on the day of Pentecost when the Holy Spirit came in like mighty rushing wind and baptized the 120 in the Upper Room with tongues like fire. Peter said, *"This is that"* (Acts 2:16).

Both Joel and Peter were prophesying by the Spirit of God that in the last days—and the last days began after Jesus ascended to the right hand of the Father—this realm would be opened to us as the Holy Spirit was poured out on believers. This gift doesn't discriminate between men and women, between young and old. The only qualification is receiving the Holy Spirit. And this gift unlocks the seer realm at new levels.

The baptism of the Holy Spirit not only positioned the apostles to work in signs, wonders, and miracles. This event opened up the eyes of believers in the early church. Stephen had an open vision of heaven (see Acts 7:56). God spoke to Ananias in a vision to visit Saul and restore his sight (see Acts 9:10–17). Paul and Peter both had visions. When you are saved and baptized in the Holy Spirit, you can operate in these realms too.

Although we know that in Jesus' name we can raise the dead, speak in tongues, heal the sick, cleanse the lepers, and cast out demons (see Matt. 10:8), and although any believer can manifest any of the spiritual gifts any time the Holy Spirit sees fit according to 1 Corinthians 12, there's a special emphasis put on prophecy over and over again—and it's connected to the outpouring of the Holy Spirit in our lives.

Pursuing Spiritual Sight

Holy Spirit's gifts are to bless people, whether saved or lost. We cannot choose to work a miracle, but we can believe in faith to walk in the miracle realm. We cannot choose to interpret tongues, but we can yield to the Holy Spirit if He chooses to give us an interpretation. Much the same, we cannot force the spirit realm open and take a peek, but we can ask the Lord to open our eyes to show us what He wants us to see, and we can walk with a sensitivity that makes us more aware of what He wants to show us.

Yes, those who have a special gift or bent to see in the spirit may see without seeking. They will see, at times, whether they want to or not.

Ezekiel, Daniel, Zechariah, John the Revelator, and others in the Bible who saw into the spirit realm did not seek supernatural experiences. God encountered them and showed them what He wanted them to see. But all can pursue the spiritual gift of seeing. In fact, twice in Scripture Paul admonishes us to pursue the gifts of the spirit.

Beyond the donkey we wrote about earlier, consider this, God opened the spirit world—the seer realm—to unbelievers in the Bible. We know Nebuchadnezzar, Pharaoh, the baker and the butler who found themselves in jail with Joseph, and Abimelech all had dreams from God warning them or showing them things to come. We know Cornelius, a non-Jewish Roman military official, had an angelic visitation that led to salvation (see Acts 10:1–8). And we know Belshazzar had a vision of a hand writing on the wall (see Dan. 5).

What's more, we see God encountering Muslims in dreams and visions unto salvation. God has not shut off the seer realm to you. You don't have to be a seer to see—and even seers can't decide to see. All believers are at God's behest when it comes to seeing in the spirit. Your part is to desires spiritual gifts and cultivate a sensitivity in your heart and a faith in your spirit to move in this gift for His glory.

Get Filled with the Spirit

You need the Holy Spirit—and you have Him. When you got saved, the Holy Spirit came to live on the inside of you. But there's a deeper immersion for you. There's more.

Jesus is the baptizer, and He wants to fill you with His Spirit to overflowing. And it's not a one-time experience. Ephesians 5:18 tells us to be filled with the Holy Spirit, but that Greek word for *filled* actually translates "being filled." In the Book of Acts we saw the apostles were filled several times—and I'm quite sure all the fillings were not chronicled.

Here are some Scriptures to build your faith in the promise of the Holy Spirit filling you:

> *If you then, evil as you are, know how to give good gifts [gifts that are to their advantage] to your children, how much more will your heavenly Father give the Holy Spirit to those who ask and continue to ask Him!* (Luke 11:13 AMPC).

> *And they were all filled (diffused throughout their souls) with the Holy Spirit and began to speak in other (different, foreign) languages (tongues), as the Spirit kept giving them clear and loud expression [in each tongue in appropriate words]* (Acts 2:4 AMPC).

> *So too the [Holy] Spirit comes to our aid and bears us up in our weakness; for we do not know what prayer to offer nor how to offer it worthily as we ought, but the Spirit Himself goes to meet our supplication and pleads in our behalf with unspeakable yearnings and groanings too deep for utterance. And He Who searches the hearts of men knows what is in the mind of the [Holy] Spirit [what His intent is], because the Spirit intercedes and pleads [before God] in behalf of the saints according to and in harmony with God's will* (Romans 8:26–27 AMPC).

Jesus is the baptizer, and He baptizes us with the Holy Spirit when we ask and believe. If you've never been filled with Spirit and you want to be—or if you want a fresh infilling—pray this prayer: "Father, I surrender full control of my life to You. I ask You even now to fill me to overflowing with Your Spirit, just as You have promised to do if I ask according to Your will. I ask this in the name of Jesus and believe that you are pouring out your Spirit upon me right now."

CHAPTER 3

THREE DIMENSIONS OF MAN

W hen it comes to mankind, there are three dimensions in one because we are created in God's image. We find these dimensions outlined in 1 Thessalonians 5:23: *"Now may the God of peace Himself sanctify you completely; and may your whole spirit, soul, and body be preserved blameless at the coming of our Lord Jesus Christ."*

Put another way, you are a spirit. You have a soul. You live in a body. Most people turn it in the opposite direction—they say body, soul, and spirit. But that is out of God's original order. You were created in His image as a spirit. The Bible puts your spirit first for good reason: God doesn't intend for you to be body led. He intends for you to be spirit led—your spirit following the leadership of Holy Spirit.

Your spirit is seated in Christ in heavenly places (see Eph. 2:6). Your soul realm is made up of your mind, will, emotions, imaginations, reasonings, and intellect. Your body is the vehicle that transports you around the earth realm, and its five senses—sight, touch, taste, smell, and hearing—engage in the physical realm.

So if two-thirds of your being is flesh and soul—and your flesh is at enmity with God (see Rom. 8:7) and your soul has yet to be fully renewed (see Rom. 12:2)—how can you consistently walk in the spirit realm? How can you condition yourself to see from a position as seated in Christ in heavenly places instead of seeing what the world, the flesh, and the devil show you as reality?

Put in a scriptural way, how do we do what Paul exhorts by the Holy Spirit's inspiration in 2 Corinthians 4:18 (AMPC): *"Since we consider and look not to the things that are seen but to the things that are unseen; for the things that are visible are temporal (brief and fleeting), but the things that are invisible are deathless and everlasting."*

Before You Begin...

Your journey into the seer dimensions begins with understanding the three parts of yourself. Armed with the knowledge of how these three dimensions operate, you will understand how God intends for you to function in the earth while simultaneously taking direction from heaven. Yes, it is possible.

Remember, you are a talking, seeing spirit with legal rights through a physical body to walk the earth. When you understand that you are a spirit—really understand this reality—you will begin to see your spiritual eyes open. When you get a revelation of how God sees you and begin to see yourself through the eyes of the spirit rather than the eyes of the soulish realm, you'll more readily recognize how each dimension of mankind ultimately affects your earthly and eternal life. This is vital to your advancement in the seer dimensions because without this key you will default to walking by faith and not by sight when you can walk by faith in your spiritual sight.

You Live in Fleshly Body

The Word commands us to obey God's spiritual laws that govern the earth dimension. Our physical body operates in the dimension called the first heaven—established in Genesis 1 when God created man out of the earth—and is governed by natural laws. Your body, for example, is subject to gravity and other laws of physics. In the first heaven, we operate through our five physical senses: taste, touch, hearing, sight, and smell. These senses inform our perception of the earth dimension around us.

From a spiritual seeing perspective, what we see in the earth dimension with your physical or naked eye is a physical manifestation that can actually be touched or communicated with or through your other senses. Your authority in this realm is predicated on your prayer and fasting life; denying your body. This is one reason why Paul the apostle wrote: *"I beseech you therefore, brethren, by the mercies of God, that you present your bodies a living sacrifice, holy, acceptable to God, which is your reasonable service"* (Rom. 12:1).

God gave us a physical body so we could be His hands and feet in the earth and execute His will. He also called us to be fruitful and multiply. Our physical bodies reproduce children who continue to populate the earth and spread His Gospel. Our physical bodies are temples for the Holy Spirit on the earth, and we are called to honor God in our bodies (see 1 Cor. 6:19–20). When we give up mortality for immorality, we are sowing our natural body and it will be raised as a spiritual body (see 1 Cor. 15:44).

Until then, our bodies—our flesh—is actually at war with the Spirit of God (see Gal. 5:17) and at enmity with God (see Rom. 8:7). The works of our flesh in Galatians 5:19–21— adultery, fornication, uncleanness, lewdness, idolatry, sorcery, hatred, contentions, jealousies, outbursts of wrath, selfish ambitions, dissensions, heresies, envy, murders, drunkenness, revelries—have to be crucified. The enemy attacks our physical bodies in the first heaven. We call it oppression. We call it sickness. We call it disease.

The good news is we are not alone in the earth dimension. God is with us and He will send angels to communicate with us in the first heaven just like He did with Jacob and others throughout the pages of the Bible (see Gen. 32:24). Sometimes angels will appear in physical form. When they do, it is always with a message from God or to partner to enhance your physical attributes to do God's will.

You Have an Unrenewed Soul

Every person has a soul. No one knows what goes on in your soul except you and God—unless you tell them. Again, your soul contains your mind, will, emotions, imaginations, reasonings, and intellect. Our soul needs to be renewed—and that renewal is a process. Inspired by the Holy Spirit, Paul wrote in Romans 12:2 (AMPC):

> *Do not be conformed to this world (this age), [fashioned after and adapted to its external, superficial customs], but be transformed (changed) by the [entire] renewal of your mind [by its new ideals and its new attitude], so that you may prove [for yourselves] what is the good and acceptable and perfect will of God, even the thing which is good and acceptable and perfect [in His sight for you].*

As your mind is renewed to the Word of God, you will gain more confidence in what you are seeing in the spirit. Many ask me how to tell the difference between their imagination and a true prophetic vision or dream. When your mind is washed with the water of the Word, you are less likely to mistake your imagination for what's truly prophetic.

Remember, John the beloved said, *"Beloved, I pray that you may prosper in all things and be in health, just as your soul prospers"* (3 John 2:2). You will see more clearly in the spirit as your soul prospers.

You Are a Spirit

You are a spirit. When you accepted Jesus, your human spirit was born again. Surely, you have heard this taught over and over again—but when you get a deeper revelation of this, it changes everything. It's the first step to being led by the Spirit into seer dimensions with greater accuracy.

See, we tend to identify more with our body our or soul for two reasons: 1) before we are born again, we rely completely on natural senses; and 2) even after we are born again, we have to train our spiritual senses and constantly sharpen them. God created mankind in His image and His likeness. As God is a Spirit, so are we. Our body is like a physical house and our souls are like computer databases that can be corrupted, which is why our minds have to be rebooted or renewed.

We connect with God spirit to Spirit. In other words, we aren't connecting with God through our mind. We don't see what He shows us in the spirit through our souls and we don't hear His voice through our physical ears (except in rare occasions of hearing the audible voice of God). We see through our spiritual eyes—the eyes of our heart—and we hear through our spiritual ears.

Our goal, then, is to develop our spirit man. While we renew our mind, we develop our spirit. We tend to spend more time on our outer man than our inner man, but Peter admonished: *"Do not let your adornment be merely outward—arranging the hair, wearing gold, or putting on fine apparel—rather let it be the hidden person of the heart, with the incorruptible beauty of a gentle and quiet spirit, which is very precious in the sight of God"* (1 Pet. 3:3-4).

We cannot enter into seer dimensions with our natural mind without risking deception. Paul wrote, *"But the natural man does not receive the things of the Spirit of God, for they are foolishness to him; nor can he know them, because they are spiritually discerned"* (1 Cor. 2:14). Just like the Old

Testament prophets spoke when the Holy Spirit moved on them, New Testament seers see as the Holy Spirit opens their eyes (see 2 Pet. 2:1).

We enter into the seer realm with our spiritual eyes and senses. If we want to see more clearly, we need to build up our spirit man. We have to let the Holy Spirit be our personal trainer, so to speak. Kenneth E. Hagin, Sr. pioneered teaching on training the human spirit and has written entire books on the topic. For our purposes, I will offer three of his points in brief, adding context as it relates to the seer dimensions.

Meditate on the Word of God

I will offer an entire chapter on meditating on the Word of God, but know that this: the Word is double-edged sword that not only divides between soul and spirit but renews your mind and educates your spirit at the same time.

Practice the Word of God

We should work to be doers of the Word. James 1:22-24 warns: "*But be doers of the word, and not hearers only, deceiving yourselves. For if anyone is a hearer of the word and not a doer, he is like a man observing his natural face in a mirror; for he observes himself, goes away, and immediately forgets what kind of man he was.*"

Jesus is the Door through whom we enter seer dimensions. Jesus is the Word made flesh. When we do not practice the Word, we are dimming our spiritual sight because our mind is deceived. When we practice the Word despite the lusts of the flesh, we are allowing our spirit man to lead and become more sensitive to seer dimensions.

Obey the Voice of Your Spirit

God speaks to our spirit and our spirit informs our conscience. Proverbs 20:27 says, "*The spirit of a man is the lamp of the Lord, searching all the inner depths of his heart.*" Since the Holy Spirit is speaking to your spirit, you should listen to your spirit. There are many instructions in the Word, but the Holy Spirit will also give you specific instructions for your life.[1]

Embracing Yourself as Three in One

One of the mysteries of God is that He is three in one, and so are we. It can be difficult to wrap your mind around that because our living condition does not always seem to match our legal position. Legally, we are seated with Christ in heavenly places. Legally, we are hidden in Christ in God. But positionally we still face warfare, sickness, grief, and toxic emotions.

Learning how to present your body as a living sacrifice and renew your mind day by day according to Romans 12:1-2 is part and parcel of letting your inner man—your spirit—lead you under the leadership of the Holy Spirit. We can only walk in the light we have (see 1 John 5:7), but we walk in more and more light as we fellowship with the Holy Spirit.

As a believer in the revelation that Christ is the Son of God, you are called to walk in heavenly places like Jesus walked. John said, *"As He is, so are we in this world* (1 John 4:17). Jesus walked with the Spirit of God everywhere He went. We can choose to do the same. Of course, this is a process—a process of faith, study, prayer, submission, and practice. But you were created to walk in these realms. You were created to see in the spirit.

CHAPTER 4

THE DREAM DIMENSION

Within the seer realm lies the dream dimension, but dreaming is not relegated to seers or even believers who see. Indeed, it's a proven scientific fact that everybody—even some animals—dreams. It seems the dream dimension fascinates people from all walks of life and all religions.

Famed psychologists Sigmund Freud and Carl Jung, among others, have attempted to explain the dream dimension and how to accurately interpret dreams and apply the interpretation to our lives. Sleep scientists have studied dreams—why we dream, when we dream, and how many times we dream—for decades. New Agers bank on dreams—often soulish dreams—to guide them in the universe.

Indeed, the world is fascinated with the images we see in our sleep.

Of course, not all dreams qualify as communication from the Holy Spirit. The enemy can bring demonic dreams—nightmares, night terrors, and night paralysis—to our souls. We can also dream carnal or soulish dreams based on the idolatry in our hearts, what we ate before bedtime, our frame of mind, or the medications we're taking. I go into much greater details about this in my book *Decoding Your Dreams*.

I can assure you of this reality: the dream realm is vital to all believers—and it's an area seers and seeing people, in particular, need to take seriously. That's because while God speaks to believers and unbelievers through dreams, dreams from seers may have broader implications than personal dreams.

Think about it. Some of the most dramatic communications we see the Lord revealing to His people—and even to heathen kings—in the Bible came in the form of dreams. God is the same yesterday, today, and forever (see Heb. 13:8). That means that to Him the dream realm is just as important a mode of communication today as it was thousands of years ago. Ignoring or taking the dream realm lightly is a mistake. You can miss God's will for your life, miss warnings for the church or world, and much more.

Distinguishing Your Dream Life

In *Decoding Your Dreams*, I shared more of dreams that were about me or pertaining to me. Upward of 90 percent of the dreams you dream will feature you as a main character. In the seer realm, though, you should expect to have dreams in which you are an observer—or dreams where you are part of something bigger than yourself.

As I have stepped deeper into this seer dimension, I've had many such dreams. I'll share a few here with some interpretation so you can see how this realm is more dramatic than your personal dream life.

This is an important distinction since as a seer or seeing person, you want to be careful to steward your own dream life, the dreams to be released to individuals pertaining to their lives (only after much intercession), and the dreams for public release intended to speak to the Body of Christ. You won't steward them rightly if you can't discern between them. I'm going to focus largely on dramatic dreams intended for the Body of Christ.

Dream of Leviathan Rising

While I was in Europe in June 2018, I had a dream that water spirits were clashing. I was looking out from a high place, like a condo with large windows overlooking the ocean. Suddenly, I saw the largest crocodile I'd ever seen in my life coming up out of the ocean with its mouth slightly open and its teeth shining. It came almost completely out of the water like a whale coming up for air.

This sight of a crocodile leaping up out of the ocean was remarkable. It was breathtaking. I was not at all scared in any way. I was just stunned. In the dream people were on the beach and they were in danger. The ocean was tumultuous like a hurricane wind was blowing. I saw other water spirits would rise up, but the crocodile was the predominant figure in the dream.

Again, the mammoth crocodile would rise up almost like a whale leaping up from the waters of the ocean. It rose up with great force and vengeance. As it rose it was wringing something in its mouth. The raging crocodile seemed to be getting pulled back down into the water as if there was an unseen struggle below the water.

At one point the crocodile was wrestling with a hippopotamus Yes, it was quite a sight. There were also serpents in the water. There was an ebb and flow of these creatures rising up out of the water, all contending with each other for supremacy. There were other animals I did not recognize. They were all reptilian in nature except the hippo. In the dream I kept trying to get people to look at what was going on, but no one was paying attention.

I write more about water spirits in my book *The Spiritual Warrior's Guide to Defeating Water Spirits*. I was familiar with these creatures through my spiritual warfare studies. But what does this really mean? First, let's look at the cast of the dream. A crocodile represents a Leviathan spirit, which is a twisting, haughty principality. A hippo represents a behemoth spirit, which is a principality that propagates ideologies such as Communism or Nazism.

This was a warning dream pertaining directly to London and more broadly Europe. These water spirits in my dream were representing principalities over regions in Europe. I did not know it at the time, but God was showing me what I would be up against when I eventually started planting Awakening House of Prayer hubs in Europe nearly a year later. He was giving me insight for me, but it was beyond me

In the dream I was looking from a high place. That symbolizes a prophetic view like a watchman. I was looking through a window, which means the demons could not get to me. I was seeing all this from my house, which can represent my ministry or my heavenly Father's house. Jesus said in Matthew 21:23, *"It is written, 'My house shall be called a house of prayer.'"*

In the dream I was trying to help, but people were not looking or willing to stop and look. The people in the dream were just oblivious to the spiritual war.

Largely, this dream is a matter of prayer and sounding the alarm to get the Body of Christ to really see what is looming over Europe. I am doing my part now as I use my Awakening House of Prayer platform to raise up watchman, intercessors, and prophets, teaching about the gifts of the spirit and spiritual warfare.

Dream of the great falling away

In another dream I was in a very high floor in a condo. This condo was not my home, but I was visiting someone else's home. Suddenly, I felt the building lean a bit forward, and I saw an entire floor of a unit above me fall, with all its contents and the people in it, down to the ground. I saw furniture falling, clothing falling, appliances falling—and people falling. It was a horrifying site. But I seemed safe.

In the dream I was not sure what to think or what to do. I wasn't panicking, but I realized everything that could be shaken was being shaken. At one point I opened the condo door and looked in the hallway. I saw a man trapped in metal that had come through the ceiling above and landed in the hallway. He was dazed, confused, and struggling to free himself.

Aghast at that sight, as well as seeing frenzied people running around the hallway, I closed and locked the door. Suddenly, the building tilted a little farther. There was another shaking. I was hunkered down because it wasn't safe to move. Then the building tilted over even farther. I wondered, "How long will it be before it collapses?"

My father was with me in the condo. He told me it was time to get out of the building. At any moment it was going to come crashing down. I was scrambling to get out the door, but I could not find two matching shoes. In the dream I felt it was important that I found matching shoes, but it was proving difficult to find the match because everything had tilted toward the window. I found two black shoes, but I wasn't satisfied. I finally found two army green colored shoes that matched and put them on my feet.

With my father, I headed down the hall toward the elevator. It seemed this was our last chance to escape. We were on the eleventh floor going down. All the buttons were pushed to stop at every floor doing down to the bottom. I was concerned that if we stopped on all those floors, we'd end up dying in the elevator. But the elevator did not stop on any floors.

When we came out, there was hustle and bustle in the lobby. Someone had set out party snacks on a table for people to eat. I thought it was odd that everyone was more interested in eating snacks than trying to get out of the shaking building. No one seemed to be overly upset. It was almost as if it was just an electrical outage or some minor issue going on. Me and my father left in safety.

This dream was really not about me. I was looking through a window, which means a prophetic view. I was first an observer in the dream but also found it as a warning of the signs of the times so I can guard my own heart and mind in Christ Jesus.

The number eleven is significant because it speaks of the eleventh hour. The eleventh hour is a symbol for the soon return of Christ. The elevator then counted down 10, 9, 8, 7, 6, 5, 4, 3, 2, 1 like NASA would count down to the launch of a space shuttle.

When we got to the lobby, they had snacks downstairs. No one seemed overly concerned even though people were dying. There was no urgency on anyone's part of get out of the building, which was clearly unstable. It was as if it was a mild power outage and there was a hurricane party going on in the lobby. As in the days of Noah, they were eating and drinking and being merry while judgment was falling.

My father in the dream represented my heavenly Father. He was leading me out of danger's way. What were the shoes about? I believe they were shoes of war, as they were military green. Not just any shoes would do. I was looking for specific shoes. Shoes speak to your walk, preparation, or authority in this context.

After much prayer, I believe this is a picture of the end-times and the great falling away and the lack of awareness of many in the church, particularly leaders. Ultimately, this depicted the fall of ministers who did not build their ministry on the Rock—on Jesus Christ. They ascended to high places, but when the shaking came, they were sifted and exposed, and lost everything in the fall. The Bible says everything that can be shaken will be shaken (see Heb. 12:27). The Bible also says judgment begins in the house of God (see 1 Pet. 4:17).

How to Enter the Dream Realm

So, how does one enter the dream realm? Can you make yourself dream? I don't believe we can make ourselves dream God-inspired dreams. There's a wave of literature on the internet about lucid dreaming that insists you can make yourself dream and that you can actually control your dreams while you sleep. Be careful about what you read on the internet.

What is lucid dreaming? As I explained in *Decoding Your Dreams*, a lucid dream is a dream in which you know you are dreaming while you are dreaming. That is rather innocent on one level, but lucid dream proponents—many of whom are New Agers—take it beyond this simple definition. They believe you can author, manipulate, shift, and turn your dreams according to your will. Maybe that's true for a soulish dream, but certainly not for a God dream.

Put another way: You may know you are dreaming a God dream, but you can't control a dream if it's coming from God any more than you can force Him to speak—and why would you want to? Remember, God dreams are God speaking to you in your dreams.

Be warned, outfits like the Lucid Dream Society offers five lucid dream techniques. This borders on witchcraft. Christians should have no desire to manipulate their mind in any way. That is the plight of the enemy. Lucid dreams, as the word describes it, falls into the realm of soulish dreams rather than the seer realm and the prophetic dream dimension.

All that said, you are probably dreaming more often than you remember. According to the National Sleep Foundation, the average adult dreams at least four to six times every night.[1] So how do we enter the dream dimension where God speaks?

Since you can't force your way into this realm—you aren't even conscious in this realm—is there anything you can do to prime the pump of your dream life? I believe there are scriptural concepts to guide is into the dream realm safely, but remember, it's up to God to speak to you in your dreams. Here are six keys to entering the dream realm:

1. Cultivate intimacy with God

God is the prophetic dream-giver, and dreams are one of His love languages. Instead of just seeking dreams, follow Christ's advice in Matthew 6:33: *"But seek first the kingdom of God and His righteousness, and all these things shall be added to you."* Although Jesus spoke these truths in the context of being concerned about natural things, such as clothing and money, the same truth applies to spiritual things.

Too often we seek the hand of God when we should be seeking the face of God. In balance, we should be seeking both His face and His hand. David wrote, *"One thing I have desired of the Lord, that will I seek: that I may dwell in the house of the Lord all the days of my life, to behold the beauty of the Lord, and to inquire in His temple"* (Ps. 27:4). When we seek to be people of one thing, we better position ourselves to receive anything He wants to give us.

2. Desire a broader dream life

There's nothing wrong with wanting to dream more. Especially for seers and seeing people, I believe this is a healthy desire. Paul said, *"Pursue love, and desire spiritual gifts, but especially that you may prophesy"* (1 Cor. 14:1). Notice here how Paul first says to *"pursue love."* God is love. God should always be our first pursuit, but we should desire spiritual gifts, especially prophetic dimensions—and that includes the seer realms.

3. Study dreams in the Bible

If you want to walk in the dream realm, study dreams in the Bible. You'll find scores of accounts of God speaking to people through dreams, offering warnings, direction, promises, and more. As you seek understanding in the Word, you are ultimately seeking God because Christ is the Word—and we know that God is a rewarder of those who diligently seek Him (see Heb. 11:6).

If God chooses, He can reward you with prophetic dreams, visions, heavenly encounters, trances, angelic visitations, and other supernatural encounters. But if we want supernatural manifestations more than we want our supernatural God, we're out of Kingdom order and opening ourselves up to deception.

4. Ask God for dreams

James gave us one key to why we don't have some things God would like to give us. "*Yet you do not have because you do not ask. You ask and do not receive, because you ask amiss, that you may spend it on your pleasures*" (James 4:2–3). Many times, God wants us to ask for something.

If you are naturally gifted as a seer or carry a seer anointing, you may not have to ask. The gift may just work. But if it's not coming naturally or if you want to go deeper into this realm, ask of the giving God. He is the giver of prophetic dreams. He is the source of the dreams we want to have.

Jesus said:

> *Ask, and it will be given to you; seek, and you will find; knock, and it will be opened to you. For everyone who asks receives, and he who seeks finds, and to him who knocks it will be opened. Or what man is there among you who, if his son asks for bread, will give him a stone? Or if he asks for a fish, will he give him a serpent? If you then, being evil, know how to give good gifts to your children, how much more will your Father who is in heaven give good things to those who ask Him!* (Matthew 7:7–11).

If you ask Him so that you can look cool or build a name for yourself, don't expect Him to answer. Ask Him with pure motives—the heart to understand more of His will, His plans, and His purposes. We know it's God's will to speak to us through dreams as one mode of communication. It's not the only way He speaks, but it's an especially common way in the Bible.

5. *Be still before you go to bed.*

If you are wound up, watching inappropriate content on TV, or otherwise unable to wind down, it can be more difficult to remember the dreams you receive from the Lord. Ecclesiastes 5:3 tells us: *"For a dream comes through much activity, and a fool's voice is known by his many words."* Still your soul by meditating on the Word or reading a godly book before you go to bed rather than adrenaline-releasing thriller movies or consuming worries.

6. *Get an impartation from a dreamer.*

Early in my Christian life I had a lot of dreams, but my dream life dried up. That can happen for many reasons, which I discuss in detail in *Decoding Your Dreams.* I remember when and how my dream life got back on track: After an impartation prayer from a dreamer named James Goll. I asked James to pray for me, and my dream life went into overdrive.

Pray this prayer: "Father, in the name of Jesus, open this dimension of the seer realm to me. Open my dream life. Help me recall, record, and remember my dreams. Help me interpret my dreams according to Your Word and Your Spirit. Help me navigate the dream realm with accuracy. Help me divide between the soul, the Spirit, and the demonic. Let me dream the dreams of God and steward them rightly for Your glory."

CHAPTER 5

THE VISION DIMENSION

I saw a veil rip from the top to bottom as I lay prostrate on the floor of my church, Awakening House of Prayer. I saw what looked like white flowing curtains, one on the left and one on the right. As I pulled the right curtains aside and peered intently behind the veil, I saw a walkway with an eclectic arrangement of bookshelves and tables on either side.

I continued looking and saw an elderly man walking circumspectly along the path. He was holding a magnifying glass. He looked something like an investigator in the Victorian Era of Great Britain but by the Spirit I knew he was more ancient. He was looking at the scrolls. He picked up a scroll, focused in with his magnifying glass, and put it away and kept walking. He did this over and over, as if he was looking for something in particular and would know when he found it.

When the vision concluded, I remained motionless on the floor. I inquired of the Lord as to what this vision meant. He showed me the investigator was looking into mysteries that became revelations to generations past—revelations recorded but lost through the ages. These books of mysteries contain revelations angels long to look into (see 1 Pet. 1:12).

On the pages of these scrolls were mysteries of the blood and mysteries of angelic forces God had unlocked to mystics, seers, and sages in the early church. Some were passed along verbally. Others were recording in writings long since lost. The Lord is waiting for a new generation to press in to unearth and uncover these revelations.

I heard the Lord say, "Who will walk through the open veil? Who will investigate the books and scrolls of the past generations and unlock ancient revelation for the present day? Who will pay the price to see? Who will clear out the eyes of the world's images and see heavenly images? There's a price to pay to see into the deep things of God."

If this encounter thrills your heart and stirs your spiritual curiosity, answer the Lord right now and say, "Here I am. Send me. Use me. Shape me. Mold me. Open my eyes to the deeper things of God."

Last Days Visions

For decades, I've heard preachers, teachers, and prophets recite and re-prophesy Peter's words from Acts 2:17-18: *"And it shall come to pass in the last days, says God, that I will pour out of My Spirit on all flesh; your sons and your daughters shall prophesy, your young men shall see visions, your old men shall dream dreams. And on My menservants and on My maidservants I will pour out My Spirit in those days; and they shall prophesy."*

If we want to enter the vision dimension accurately, we should be students of what scripture says about visions so we can plumbline what we see against the inerrant Word of God. Let's start off with the basic question: "What is a vision?"

The Hebrew word for vision is *chazah*, which means "vision, a sight (mentally), i.e. a dream, revelation, or oracle—vision," according to *Strong's Concordance. Brown-Driver-Briggs* breaks it down as a "vision, as seen in an ecstatic state," "vision, in the night," and "divine communication in a vision, oracle, prophecy."[1]

The Greek word for vision is *horasis*, which means "the act of seeing, a vision, appearance," according to the *NAS Exhaustive Concordance.*

Thayer's Greek Lexicon defines vision as "the act of seeing; the sense of sight; appearance, visible form, a vision, i.e., an appearance divinely granted in an ecstasy." And *Strong's Exhaustive Concordance* defines vision as "the act of gazing, i.e. (externally) an aspect or (internally) an inspired appearance—a sight, vision."[2]

Simply put, you dream while you are asleep. You have visions when you are awake. You can have a vision within a dream but ultimately a vision within a dream is still part of the dream dimension. In all cases, Holy Spirit-inspired visions are one more way God communicates with His people. God-given visions are supernatural revelations—divine communication—from heaven.

Three General Types of Visions

There are categories of visions just as there are categories of dreams. There are three overarching types of prophetic visions—pictures, trances, and open visions. Within these three categories some use different language, such as inner visions, night visions, apocalyptic visions, panoramic visions, and the like. Ultimately, though, they fall into three classifications. Let's look at each:

1. Pictures: In prophetic circles, you may hear people say they are seeing a picture. These are visual impressions or images that often arise when praying over someone or even in your own private prayer time. The Holy Spirit shows you a visual. It may just be a flash. On my "Mornings with the Holy Spirit" prayer broadcasts on Facebook, I often see pictures as I pray. In one deliverance-oriented vision, I saw people bound up with rope. When I looked closer, I saw the rope had the word "past" written all over it. Don't discount the flashes and quick

pictures the Holy Spirit shows you. It could be life-changing for someone.

2. Trances: A trance is a state of one who is "out of himself," according to *Easton's Bible Dictionary*. The word *trance* comes from the Greek word *ekstasis*, from which the word *ecstasy* is derived. Peter fell into a trance in Acts 10:10 that opened his eyes to preach the gospel to the Gentiles. Paul fell into a trance in Acts 22:17 in which the Lord gave him a warning and a commission to preach the gospel to the Gentiles. I suppose it's hard to describe it if you've not experienced it. We'll talk more about trances in a later chapter.

3. Open vision: Open visions appear to you like a movie or imagery acting out before your very eyes. Your eyes are open and you are immune to what is going on around you. It's like the word around you stops. Paul had an open vision on the road to Damascus (see Acts 9:3-9) and also in the night when he received the Macedonian call (Acts 16:9).

Dramatic Biblical Visions

The Bible offers accounts of massively dramatic visions that are worthy of study. Dramatic visions did not end in the Bible. Rick Joyner has had some dramatic visions that he published in books. One of them, *Final Quest*, is a panoramic vision of the ultimate quest—the last battle between light and darkness. The late David Wilkerson had a prophetic vision about doomsday that has gone around the world. These and the biblical examples below should make us hungry to move deeper into this seer dimension. Let's look at a few of the dramatic Old Testament visions.

Ezekiel's Open Vision

> *Then I looked, and behold, a whirlwind was coming out of the north, a great cloud with raging fire engulfing itself; and brightness was all around it and radiating out of its midst like the color of amber, out of the midst of the fire. Also from within it came the likeness of four living creatures. And this was their appearance: they had the likeness of a man. Each one had four faces, and each one had four wings. Their legs were straight, and the soles of their feet were like the soles of calves' feet. They sparkled like the color of burnished bronze. The hands of a man were under their wings on their four sides; and each of the four had faces and wings. Their wings touched one another. The creatures did not turn when they went, but each one went straight forward* (Ezekiel 1:4-9).

This vision continues through the first chapter, and Ezekiel had other profound visions as well.

Zechariah's Eight Night Visions

> *I saw by night, and behold, a man riding on a red horse, and it stood among the myrtle trees in the hollow; and behind him were horses: red, sorrel, and white. Then I said, "My lord, what are these?" So the angel who talked with me said to me, "I will show you what they are." And the man who stood among the myrtle trees answered and said, "These are the ones whom the Lord has sent to walk to and fro throughout the earth." So they answered the Angel of the Lord, who stood among the myrtle trees, and said, "We have walked to and fro throughout the earth, and behold, all the earth is resting quietly"* (Zechariah 1:8-11).

Zachariah's night visions run from Zechariah 1:8–6:15.

Daniel's Apocalyptic Visions

> *Now on the twenty-fourth day of the first month, as I was by the side of the great river, that is, the Tigris, I lifted my eyes and looked, and behold, a certain man clothed in linen, whose waist was girded with gold of Uphaz! His body was like beryl, his face like the appearance of lightning, his eyes like torches of fire, his arms and feet like burnished bronze in color, and the sound of his words like the voice of a multitude.*
>
> *And I, Daniel, alone saw the vision, for the men who were with me did not see the vision; but a great terror fell upon them, so that they fled to hide themselves. Therefore I was left alone when I saw this great vision, and no strength remained in me; for my vigor was turned to frailty in me, and I retained no strength. Yet I heard the sound of his words; and while I heard the sound of his words I was in a deep sleep on my face, with my face to the ground* (Daniel 10:4-9).

Daniel is often called a book of visions because of the many visions the Lord gave him. The passage above is just one example.

Visions did not stop in the Old Testament. In the New Testament, we see Ananias, Paul, Peter, and Cornelius had prophetic visions. The Book of Revelation is a dramatic vision of the end times worthy of study.

Developing the Seer Gift for Visions

You can prophesy according to the proportion of your faith, but you can't have a dream or a vision according to the proportion of your faith (see Rom. 12:6). In other words, you can have demonic dreams our carnal dreams but you can't decide to have God dreams or a God vision in the same way we prophesy verbally by an unction. You can, however, develop the seer anointing in your life. Here are 15 ways:

1. *"Zelo" to See What God Wants to Show You*

The Bible says, *"Pursue love, and desire spiritual gifts, but especially that you may prophesy"* (1 Cor. 14:1). Remember, the word for "desire" in the Greek is *zelo*. According to *The KJV New Testament Greek Lexicon*, it's a pretty intense feeling. It means to burn with zeal; in a good sense, to be zealous in the pursuit of good; desire earnestly; and pursue. *Merriam-Webster* defines zeal as "a strong feeling of interest and enthusiasm that makes someone very eager or determined to do something."

2. *Cast Down Vain Imaginations and Yield to Prophetic Imaginations*

You need to clear your mind of the vain imaginations the devil and your carnal nature inspires to make more head room for the prophetic imaginations—the dreams and visions the Lord wants to share. Get rid of the clutter! Paul wrote, *"Casting down imaginations, and every high thing that exalteth itself against the knowledge of God, and bringing into captivity every thought to the obedience of Christ"* (2 Cor. 10:5 KJV).

3. *Exercise Your Holy Imagination*

God gave you an imagination. You can exercise it for good or evil. Before the flood, *"God saw that the wickedness of man was great in the earth, and that every imagination of the thoughts of his heart was only evil continually"* (Gen. 6:5 KJV). But we can also use our imagination for good. Paul wrote about *"him that is able to do exceeding abundantly above all that we ask or think, according to the power that worketh in us"* (Eph. 3:20 KJV). Imagine the Scripture scenes in your mind. Imagine the dramatic visions in your mind. Imagine God on His throne. Stretch your holy imagination.

4. *Study Visions in the Bible*

Study the visions in the Bible to understand vision language. In doing so, you're studying how the gift operates in living color. The Word of God is alive. Studying the visions in the Bible will make you more open to receiving visions. It may start with small pictures at first and you may never have the dramatic visions of Ezekiel, but it will position your heart with hunger to receive.

5. *Guard Your Eye Gates*

We have to be cautious about what we set our eyes upon because it can defile our spiritual vision. Consider these scriptures:

- Psalm 101:3: *"I will set nothing wicked before my eyes."*
- Matthew 6:22: *"The lamp of the body is the eye. If therefore your eye is good, your whole body will be full of light."*
- Matthew 5:29: *"If your right eye causes you to sin, pluck it out and cast it from you; for it is more profitable for you that one of your members perish, than for your whole body to be cast into hell."*

6. *Ask the Lord for Visions*

The Holy Spirit distributes spiritual gifts as He wills (see 1 Cor. 12:11), but it can't hurt to ask.

7. *Meditate on The Promise of Visions*

Joel 2:28-29 promises, *"And it shall come to pass afterward that I will pour out My Spirit on all flesh; your sons and your daughters shall prophesy, your old men shall dream dreams, your young men shall see visions. And also on My menservants and on My maidservants I will pour out My Spirit in those days."* Renew your mind to the reality that the Lord will keep His promise in these last days.

8. *Pursue Intimacy with God*

Even when David was on the run from Saul, he found time to spend with God (see Ps. 57).

Jesus, the strong Son of God, set time apart with the Father consistently in the Gospels (see Mark 1:35; 14:32-34; Matthew 14:13; Luke 4:42; 5:16; 6:12; John 6:15).

9. *Purify Your Motives*

Every prophetic release should be motivated by love. If it's not motivated by love it's not coming from God because God is love. *"If I have the gift of prophecy, and understand all mysteries and all knowledge, and if I have all faith, so that I could remove mountains, and have not love, I am nothing"* (1 Cor. 13:2 MEV).

10. *Read Books About the Seer Gift*

James Goll's book *The Seer* is one of the best books out there. Read books by reputable leaders on this gift. Beware of some goofy New Age stuff on the Internet, as well as books written by people who have an unseasoned gift and who could be teaching prematurely. Track records are important.

11. *Steward What You See*

"Moreover it is required in stewards that a man be found faithful" (1 Cor. 4:2 MEV). Everything belongs to the Lord. He is the giver of visions and the interpreter of them. We need to be faithful to steward the visions He gives us. Write them down, pray into them, meditate on them, etc.

12. *Press in to Symbolic Language*

Visions are often more literal than dreams but they, too, can be full of symbols. Study the symbolism in the Bible so you can understand what God is saying.

13. *Judge What You See*

We'll talk more about this in the section below, but it's important to judge any supernatural revelation. Not all supernatural experiences come from God.

14. Pray Out What You See

Pray into the vision you've received to understand what the Lord wants you to do with it, how you should apply it, and whether you should share it. This is part of stewarding the vision.

15. Act on What You See

Sometimes you need to take specific actions according to a vision you see. Act in faith on the vision when the Lord has made it clear.

Testing Your Visual Accuracy

Your holy imagination might show you a picture—even a good picture—but it doesn't mean it's a God picture. There are a lot of good things in your mind and your spirit that aren't necessarily coming from God. It's important to test your visual accuracy in the spirit just as you would in the natural. If your natural vision is not strong, you need a prescription to fix it. If your spiritual vision is dim or you are seeing wrongly, the prescription is the Word and the Spirit.

The Lord speaks of prophets who *"prophesy lies in My name. I have not sent them, commanded them, nor spoken to them; they prophesy to you a false vision, divination, a worthless thing, and the deceit of their heart"* (Jer. 14:14). And again, *"Do not listen to the words of the prophets who prophesy to you. They make you worthless; they speak a vision of their own heart, not from the mouth of the Lord"* (Jer. 23:16).

I believe these were false prophets offering knowingly false visions. In your case, you are working to discern whether what you are seeing is from the Lord or just your imagination running wild—or even the wicked one. A vision from God will not violate Scripture but should somehow glorify God by showing you His will, revealing the enemy's plans, or spurring you to press into Him or pray. I'll share specific ways people fall into seer deception in the final chapter.

CHAPTER 6

THE ANGELIC DIMENSION

I have never seen an angel face to face, but I have seen them pass by many times—and many people tell me they see angels standing on either side of me as I minister.

My angelic encounters may not be as dramatic as yours, but they are just as real. There are degrees of seeing in the spirit. Discerning of spirits and feeling go hand in hand with the seer realm. So as someone who operates under a seer anointing, I have had my fair share of incidents with angels, which are ministering spirits sent to minister to the heirs of salvation (see Heb. 1:14).

Angels perform many functions, but the word *angel* itself means "messenger," so whatever other functions angels perform, they typically bring some sort of message—even if it is just their presence that communicates God's love, power, and comfort to your heart.

When I was in Singapore some years ago, I woke up in my hotel room and discerned a war in the spirit. I knew there were demons present, and I knew there were angels present. I began to worship and war at the same time. I had a sense of urgency in my heart. I was praying without ceasing in the spirit, then the room calmed.

What happened? There was indeed a spiritual war in my hotel room. I felt the presence of the Holy Spirit and God's holy angels. That's when an angel of revelation arrived, and the Holy Spirit gave me instruction. I've been walking in new levels of revelation ever since. On an earlier trip to Singapore, the Lord told me He was sending me back to the states with angels of fire. I haven't personally seen them, but I know they are with me because of the power and fire manifestations that have accompany my ministry.

I've also met angels unaware. I came out of a restaurant with my daughter one evening, and what appeared to be a homeless person approached me for money to buy food. I didn't have any cash, so I apologized and headed to my car. I suddenly realized I could give the person the food I hadn't touched from the dinner. I turned around to offer the food—literally two seconds later—and the person was nowhere to be found.

That reminds me of Hebrews 13:2: *"Be not forgetful to entertain strangers: for thereby some have entertained angels unawares"* (KJV). That word *unawares* comes from the Greek word *lanthano.* According to the King James Version New Testament Greek lexicon, it means "to be hidden, to be hidden from one, secretly, unawares, without knowing."[1]

In discussing angels in the unseen realm, we must understand angels are not limited to the spirit realm. Angels do not have the same restrictions as demons regarding operating in the earth. Demons need a body to navigate the earth realm—they must oppress or possess a human or an animal to operate legally in the earth. God can send angels on assignment, and they can manifest in human form without possessing someone's body.

We're coming into contact with angels more than we know. As seers and seeing believers, we can only see angels God wants to show us. They hide from our view until the Lord allows them to reveal themselves. At the same time, I believe we are missing angelic manifestations because our eyes have not been trained to see.

God Can Open Our Eyes to the Angelic

Angels visited men and women in the Old and New Testaments. Sometimes it was through dreams and visions. Other times it was in human form. Angelic encounters—whether in the seen or unseen realm—did not come to a screeching halt after the Bible was canonized. Remember, God is the same yesterday, today, and forever (see Heb. 13:8).

Although some naysayers and cesassionists insist that the fifteen people in the Bible who saw angels do not mean we all have the ability see angels, we have to understand that only fifteen encounters were recorded. It's likely that others saw angels in their many manifestations. In fact, it was so common to see angels in Bible times that when Peter was released from prison, the intercessors who had stayed up all night to pray without ceasing for him thought an angel was knocking on the door. Consider this scene in Acts 12:5–16:

> *Peter was therefore kept in prison, but constant prayer was offered to God for him by the church. And when Herod was about to bring him out, that night Peter was sleeping, bound with two chains between two soldiers; and the guards before the door were keeping the prison. Now behold, an angel of the Lord stood by him, and a light shone in the prison; and he struck Peter on the side and raised him up, saying, "Arise quickly!" And his chains fell off his hands. Then the angel said to him, "Gird yourself and tie on your sandals"; and so he did. And he said to him, "Put on your garment and follow me." So he went out and followed him, and did not know that what was done by the angel was real, but thought*

he was seeing a vision. When they were past the first and the second guard posts, they came to the iron gate that leads to the city, which opened to them of its own accord; and they went out and went down one street, and immediately the angel departed from him.

And when Peter had come to himself, he said, "Now I know for certain that the Lord has sent His angel, and has delivered me from the hand of Herod and from all the expectation of the Jewish people."

So, when he had considered this, he came to the house of Mary, the mother of John whose surname was Mark, where many were gathered together praying. And as Peter knocked at the door of the gate, a girl named Rhoda came to answer. When she recognized Peter's voice, because of her gladness she did not open the gate, but ran in and announced that Peter stood before the gate. But they said to her, "You are beside yourself!" Yet she kept insisting that it was so. So they said, "It is his angel."

Now Peter continued knocking; and when they opened the door and saw him, they were astonished.

Think about it for a minute. The angel rescues Peter. He knows it's an angelic encounter, but he's not sure if it's really happening or if it's just a vision. This is consistent with Paul's account of his visit to heaven in 2 Corinthians 12:3–4: *"And I know such a man—whether in the body or out of the body I do not know, God knows—how he was caught up into Paradise and heard inexpressible words, which it is not lawful for a man to utter."* Sometimes you're just not sure what or how you've seen in the spirit realm.

But the larger point is that the intercessors were astonished it was Peter. They had more faith to believe it was an angel—they had more faith that it was Peter's angel—even though they had entered effective, fervent prayer for the apostle. That tells you just how common angelic sightings were in Bible days. I very much doubt that all those intercessors were seers or even carried a seer anointing, per se, but they were accustomed to seeing angels.

How much more so now, especially among seers and seeing people. Joel prophesied God would pour out His Spirit on all flesh in the last days. That prophesied outpouring was re-prophesied after the Day of Pentecost. Peter affirmed Joel's prophesy was happening now. Since the Holy Spirit came to live in believers, we have even greater access to the seer realm because, as we discussed in an earlier chapter, the Holy Seer lives on the inside of us.

How Angels Manifest

How did angels manifest in the Bible? It's important to note that angels in Scripture do not appear as winged creatures or as female. Female winged-creations in Zechariah 5:9 were not called angels, but winged creatures. Let's look at some biblical examples to build our faith.

We know Gideon saw an angel of the Lord, who called him a mighty man of valor (see Judg. 6:12). Elisha prayed for the Lord to open the eyes of his very frightened servant so he could see into the spirit realm. What did he see? The mountain was full of horses and chariots of fire surrounding them (see 2 Kings 6:17). His servant saw the Lord's angel armies. When Jacob was preparing to meet his estranged brother Esau, whose birthright he stole, Jacob saw the angels of God (see Gen. 32:1). But we have more specifics about how angels manifest to our natural and spiritual eyes.

Angels manifest as humans.

Lot saw two angels while he was sitting at the gate of Sodom:

> *Now the two angels came to Sodom in the evening, and Lot*
> *was sitting in the gate of Sodom. When Lot saw them, he rose*
> *to meet them, and he bowed himself with his face toward the*
> *ground. And he said, "Here now, my lords, please turn in to*
> *your servant's house and spend the night, and wash your feet;*
> *then you may rise early and go on your way"* (Gen. 19:1–2).

These angels appeared as humans, but somehow Lot discerned they were angels. Genesis 18:2, Judges 13:6, Mark 16:5, and Luke 24:4 also show angels manifesting as humans. In this case, you don't need spiritual eyes to see them, but you do need spiritual discernment to really see them.

With hundreds of thousands of believers in America crying out for mercy in accordance with 2 Chronicles 7:14—*"If My people who are called by My name will humble themselves, and pray and seek My face, and turn from their wicked ways, then I will hear from heaven, and will forgive their sin and will heal their land."*—an angelic encounter in our nation's capital spoke hope and life in a pivotal hour.

Dutch Sheets, an international best-selling author and conference speaker, shares: "In February while praying at the White House, two friends and I had an angelic visitation. In response to our prayers and decrees, the angel simply said, 'Mercy, mercy, mercy, mercy, mercy, mercy.' Yes, six times."[2] The timing was just months before the 2016 US presidential election—and before Donald Trump won the Republican nomination.

In this case, as Dutch describes the encounter, the angel appeared in human form. The angel walked toward them, then right by them as he repeated "mercy" six times. The angel disappeared almost as quickly as he appeared. This is a good example of an angelic manifestation according to Hebrews 13:2 cited previously. One reason you may entertain angels unknowingly is because they may appear to you in human form.

Angels can manifest as flaming fire.

Moses saw an angel in the form of a flaming fire in the midst of a bush:

> *Now Moses was tending the flock of Jethro his father-in-law, the priest of Midian. And he led the flock to the back of the desert, and came to Horeb, the mountain of God. And the Angel of the Lord appeared to him in a flame of fire from the midst of a bush. So he looked, and behold, the bush was burning with fire, but the bush was not consumed* (Exodus 3:1–2).

Hebrews 1:7 and Psalm 104:4 both describe angels as flames of fire.

Angels can manifest as spiritual beings.

Hagar saw an angel by a spring of water in the desert in a moment of desperation (see Gen. 16:7). A donkey saw an angel of the Lord with a sword drawn in His hand (see Num. 22:23). Balaam, who was riding the donkey also saw Him (see Num. 22:31).

Angels can manifest as wind.

The blowing of wind can point to angelic activity. Psalm 104:4 says God *"makes his angels winds"* (NHEB).

Bethel Redding posted this story:

> A man named Al Chadwick has been colorblind and dyslexic; he is 54. He was at work last Tuesday and felt a heavenly presence. He looked around and saw seven angels on a nearby ridge with their swords drawn. One of the angels waved at him, and he waved back. He thought, "Hey, that's kind of cool. I get to hang out with angels."
>
> He felt a wind and looked up, but there was no wind. There was an angel standing next to him. The angel said,

"You are blessed. Be healed" and touched his forehead. He noticed that there were three different shades of brown on the mountains where he was. He noticed that he could see color. He used to see differently. Yellow looked almost white. Purple didn't look quite right. He saw mostly black, white, and gray and shades between.

It was difficult because when he drove through a traffic light, he had to look closely to see what was lit. He used to have trouble seeing at night. Now he can see at night, and he can see colors. God gave him a gift to release blessing on people. He told him to bless a friend, and the next day he went to his friend to pronounce blessings on him. His friend asked him about his bad dyslexia and gave him something to read. The words were perfect. He said, "God double-dipped me, and I didn't even know it. God is in a good mood!"[3]

Angels can manifest as light.

Angels have also appeared in brilliance or light. Ezekiel 1:13, Daniel 10:6, Matthew 28:3, and Acts:1:10 are all examples.

In his book *Angel Armies: Releasing the Warriors of Heaven*, Tim Sheets tells the story of ministering at a church in Jacksonville, Florida. He arrived late, but when he walked in he sensed God's supernatural activity was stirring in the worship service.

As I walked from the back to the front of the auditorium, I began to see flashes of light going back and forth across the congregation. I stopped I my tracks because, as I have taught, that refers to angelic activity. Angels were moving all around the auditorium, ministering to God's people.... The next morning began as the worship leader opened with a song to gather everyone together and prepare their minds for receiving mode. My brother, Dutch Sheets, opened the service in prayer. I stood there on the front row, getting ready to minister, when I saw, off to the right, a group of angels. To the left there was a group of angels stationed as well. They were angel warriors. I looked up and saw angel warriors stationed everywhere![4]

This, of course, was enough to capture his attention but even more so because something similar had happened a few months before in New York. Sheets reports seeing two bands of angels on each side of those who had responded to the altar call. Cindy Jacobs had called up teenagers and adults up to the age of thirty for prayer.

"While we were praying, I heard, called out from behind me, 'Mahanaim.' I know exactly what *Mahanaim* is because I teach about it. Of course, God knew that word would grab my attention and I would recognize it meant the Angel of the Lord who accompanies the apostolic assignment on my life. Finally I looked to see who was yelling, "Mahanaim." To my surprise, there was nobody behind me. I began to shake internally."

Mahanaim is a Hebrew word found in Genesis 32. Jacob left Laban to return home and was going to meet his brother Esau, whose birthright he stole. Scripture records Jacob witnessing two groups of angels protecting his family. Jacob called that place Mahanaim, which means "two camps," according to *Strong's Concordance*.[5]

"Back to the meeting in Jacksonville: I remembered what I had seen in New York and what I read in Genesis....I saw the same thing and I knew the Holy Spirit was using the angels to protect what He is doing with the coming generation—particularly that night, what He was doing with the youth in that church....I have now had two encounters with *Mahanaim*, seeing them surround, as guards, the next generation."[6]

James Goll, author of *Angelic Encounters: Engaging Help from Heaven,* says we shouldn't just expect angelic visitations to increase in the near future—we should expect it now. Like his contemporaries, he already sees an increase of angelic activity in the earth today.

"Angels of His presence is one of the primary categories of angels that have and are being released. That is part of the reason why there is such an increase of the manifested presence of God in our worship services," Goll says. "Yes, this tangible presence of God is a dimension of the Holy Spirit. But in many places there is another level that is already upon us. His presence is intensifying because we are drawing angels themselves to come and join in with us in our worship and praise."

Goll describes the manifestation of angelic visitation in several ways. One is an atmosphere "getting thicker." Another is increased anointings. Yet another is spontaneous healings happening as we extravagantly enter into worship and praise. That, he says, is because angels are worshipping with us, but they are also ministering to us. That is part of their job description, according to Hebrews 1:14.

"Do you feel the fire of His presence increasing? Do you feel an actual wind blowing? Are healings happening without anyone laying hands on anyone? If that is the case, then the Heavenly Host has just joined you…and they are releasing the Kingdom of God in our midst. In His Kingdom there is His rule and reign," Goll says. "The King sits and He reigns. We then experience a heightened awareness of angelic activity and a super-charged atmosphere of faith where all things are possible."

Angels Break and Bend Light Barriers

Oftentimes people see angels as flashes of light. Why do angels manifest as flashes of light? Because they travel faster than the speed of light, they are actually breaking the light barrier. You may have heard of the sound barrier. When you break it, you hear a sonic boom, which NASA defines as "the thunder-like noise a person on the ground hears when an aircraft or other type of aerospace vehicle flies overhead faster than the speed of sound."[7] It's called supersonic.

But what is the light barrier? Scientifically speaking, it's the theoretical maximum speed at which any physical object or information can travel—it's the speed of light. But since angels travel faster than the speed of light, they break the light barrier and manifest as various colors. Often, people see angels as white light, but many have reported seeing angels in many different colors.

Warning: All Angelic Visitations Are Not Real

Although angels can visit, we have to fall back on the Bible to judge supernatural experiences. Second Timothy 3:16–17 tells us: *"All Scripture is inspired by God and is profitable for teaching, for reproof, for correction, and for instruction in righteousness, that the man of God may be complete, thoroughly equipped for every good work"* (MEV).

At the end of the day we must maintain our focus on the God of the angels rather than the angels themselves. If we obsess over angelic visitations, we will find ourselves out of balance and open a door for the enemy to bring deception to our minds. I don't see anywhere in Scripture where people fervently sought out angelic visitations.

We cannot decide to have an angelic visitation any more than we can decide to have a spectacular vision. God may choose to send an angel to offer direction, but angels should not replace the leadership of the Holy Spirit in our lives. When we put more emphasis on angels than we do Father, Son, and Holy Spirit, we're ripe for deadly error. Indeed, entire religions have been founded based on revelations from angels. Cults have risen up based on a man's or woman's experience with an angel.

How to See Angels

Ultimately, God has to open your eyes to angels. You can't make them manifest, and asking them to appear won't do you any good because they obey the will of the Lord. You can position your heart to be more sensitive to the presence of angels.

Practice discernment.

Many of us are hardwired to discern demons, but our gift of discernment—which is connected to the seer realm—should also work to discern the Holy Spirit and angels. Learn how your gift of discernment works. Feelers may sense a peace or love in the atmosphere or get goosebumps when angels are present. Audible discerners may just hear the Lord telling them angels are there. You might see a light or feel heat or wind.

Be spiritually alert.

Be intentional about staying spiritually alert.

Pray in the spirit.

When you pray in the spirit, you build yourself up in your most holy faith (see Jude 20). Praying in the spirit makes you more sensitive to the Holy Spirit.

Enter into intercession.

Intercession can be a gateway to open your eyes and your ears to the spirit realm. Intercession is selfless as you are not praying for yourself but for others. When you pray or make intercession, often it will unleash a war in the heavens like it did in Daniel's day. When Daniel prayed, an angel was sent to bring the answer, but the prince of Persia withstood him. Michael the archangel had to step into the battle (see Dan. 10). God may allow you, like he did Tim Sheets, to see that battle.

Ask for a fresh infilling.

Christians are little leaky sometimes. Ask the Holy Spirit to fill you again so that you can maximize your sensitivity to Him. You may be somewhat sensitive to a light sprinkle of rain, for example, but you'll be very sensitive to a monsoon.

Ask God to show you angels.

You can ask God to open your eyes to the angelic realm. This is scriptural since Elisha asked the Lord on behalf of his servant. The Lord may or may not answer this prayer, or He may not answer it immediately. God won't show you angels without a purpose just because you ask. His purpose could be to train your eyes or just to bless you because of your genuine curiosity. But He's not going to open a game of hide-and-seek for you with the heavenly host.

CHAPTER 7

THE HEAVENLY DIMENSION

H eaven is for real. We know that because the pages of Scripture give us dramatic accounts of this realm. Amazon lists over twenty thousand books on the topic of heaven, some of which offer the chronicles of personal encounters and everyday Joes like we have recorded. Others work to prove heaven exists. Still others focus on the new heaven and the new earth.

The late minister Charles Ferguson Ball once said, "Heaven is a place, just as much a place as New York or Chicago."[1] Interestingly, in a LifeWay Research study 64 percent of people with evangelical beliefs say people will ultimately be reunited with their loved ones in heaven, and 54 percent say only those who trust in Jesus as their Savior receive God's free gift of eternal salvation.[2] It's no wonder we see heavenly encounters increasing. It's almost as if God is trying to wake up not only the world, but also the church.

Yes, heaven is a real place. Jesus calls heaven a place twice in two passages of Scripture. In John 14:1–3, He said: *"Let not your heart be troubled; you believe in God, believe also in Me. In My Father's house are many mansions; if it were not so, I would have told you. I go to prepare a place for you. And if I go and prepare a place for you, I will come again and receive you to Myself; that where I am, there you may be also.”*

Heaven is where God dwells. It is His permanent residence. His throne is stationed in heaven. Angels have their home base there, ascending and descending to the second heaven and the earth realm at His command (Scripture). Jesus Christ is seated at the right hand of our Father who is in heaven. And although we find ourselves walking in a temporal realm that will one day perish—and we may carry passports from any number of nations depending upon where we were born—our actual citizenship is in heaven (see Phil. 3:20).

In Revelation 21 we see heaven as a massive city with a great population. Hebrews 11:10 speaks of heaven as a city God designed and built Himself. Hebrews 11:16 calls heaven *“a better country”* (NIV). In Luke 23:43, Jesus refers to heaven as paradise. We’ve been conditioned to believe heaven is a place we go to when we die, and many believers are there now. According to Philippians 1:21–23, that is partially true. But can seers and seeing people—any believer in covenant with God and even unbelievers—have encounters with the heavenly realm?

We often think of heaven as a place that is situated somewhere beyond Pluto. We see it as a nebulous and mysterious. But heaven is not somewhere off in the distance, light years away in another galaxy. Heaven is just beyond the veil. If God is omnipresent—which is He— then heaven can’t too far away at any given moment. If the Kingdom of God is within us—which it is—then heaven is closer than religion has trained us to think.

What Is Heaven Really Like?

God created heaven (see Gen. 1:1). The Bible speaks of the gate of heaven (see Gen. 28:17). There will be no more death, mourning, crying, or pain in heaven (see Rev. 21:4). There is a throne room in heaven (see Rev. 3:12;

4:1). You can do an in-depth study on heaven and many books have. Four our purposes of the seer realms, the Book of Revelation gives us some awesome insights into heaven's appearance. Revelation 4 gives us details of heaven and its operations:

> *After these things I looked, and behold, a door standing open in heaven. And the first voice which I heard was like a trumpet speaking with me, saying, "Come up here, and I will show you things which must take place after this."*
>
> *Immediately I was in the Spirit; and behold, a throne set in heaven, and One sat on the throne. And He who sat there was like a jasper and a sardius stone in appearance; and there was a rainbow around the throne, in appearance like an emerald. Around the throne were twenty-four thrones, and on the thrones I saw twenty-four elders sitting, clothed in white robes; and they had crowns of gold on their heads. And from the throne proceeded lightnings, thunderings, and voices. Seven lamps of fire were burning before the throne, which are the seven Spirits of God.*
>
> *Before the throne there was a sea of glass, like crystal. And in the midst of the throne, and around the throne, were four living creatures full of eyes in front and in back. The first living creature was like a lion, the second living creature like a calf, the third living creature had a face like a man, and the fourth living creature was like a flying eagle. The four living creatures, each having six wings, were full of eyes around and within. And they do not rest day or night, saying:*
>
> *"Holy, holy, holy, Lord God Almighty, Who was and is and is to come!"*
>
> *Whenever the living creatures give glory and honor and thanks to Him who sits on the throne, who lives forever and*

ever, the twenty-four elders fall down before Him who sits on the throne and worship Him who lives forever and ever, and cast their crowns before the throne, saying:

"You are worthy, O Lord, to receive glory and honor and power; for You created all things, and by Your will they exist and were created."

And Revelation 21:9–25 offers the most in-depth description of heaven in the Bible:

Then one of the seven angels who had the seven bowls filled with the seven last plagues came to me and talked with me, saying, "Come, I will show you the bride, the Lamb's wife." And he carried me away in the Spirit to a great and high mountain, and showed me the great city, the holy Jerusalem, descending out of heaven from God, having the glory of God. Her light was like a most precious stone, like a jasper stone, clear as crystal. Also she had a great and high wall with twelve gates, and twelve angels at the gates, and names written on them, which are the names of the twelve tribes of the children of Israel: three gates on the east, three gates on the north, three gates on the south, and three gates on the west.

Now the wall of the city had twelve foundations, and on them were the names of the twelve apostles of the Lamb. And he who talked with me had a gold reed to measure the city, its gates, and its wall. The city is laid out as a square; its length is as great as its breadth. And he measured the city with the reed: twelve thousand furlongs. Its length, breadth, and height are equal. Then he measured its wall: one hundred and forty-four cubits, according to the measure of a man, that is, of an angel. The construction of its wall was of jasper; and the city was pure gold, like clear glass. The foundations of the wall of the city were adorned with all kinds of precious stones: the first foundation was jasper, the second sapphire, the third chalcedony, the fourth emerald, the fifth sardonyx, the sixth sardius, the seventh chrysolite, the eighth beryl, the ninth topaz, the tenth chrysoprase, the eleventh jacinth, and the twelfth amethyst. The twelve gates were twelve pearls: each individual gate was of one pearl. And the street of the city was pure gold, like transparent glass.

But I saw no temple in it, for the Lord God Almighty and the Lamb are its temple. The city had no need of the sun or of the moon to shine in it, for the glory of God illuminated it. The Lamb is its light. And the nations of those who are saved shall walk in its light, and the kings of the earth bring their glory and honor into it. Its gates shall not be shut at all by day (there shall be no night there).

The Fruit of Heaven Encounters

I have never encountered heaven, but I know people who have. Some, like Patricia King, are among us today. Others, like Bob Jones, have gone home to be with the Lord. When God allows man to enter into heaven before the first death, He does so with a purpose. This is an important point because, in today's church, many claim to go to heaven, but the fruit of their experience is lacking. Everything God does is purposeful. If He allows you to see or enter the heavenly realm, there's a reason behind such a dramatic event.

There are many reasons God may allow someone to see or even enter heaven before they die. Some believers come back with details that prove the reality of heaven and its inhabitants so as to stir the faith of others to believe. Sometimes it's to send a message back to earth. Some things, though, God does not want us to share. We see this concept with both Daniel and Paul. Daniel saw the throne room of God but was told to seal the scroll on which he wrote about his encounter (see Dan. 12:4). Paul explained:

> *It is doubtless not profitable for me to boast. I will come to visions and revelations of the Lord: I know a man in Christ who fourteen years ago—whether in the body I do not know, or whether out of the body I do not know, God knows—such a one was caught up to the third heaven. And I know such a man—whether in the body or out of the body I do not know, God knows—how he was caught up into Paradise and heard inexpressible words, which it is not lawful for a man to utter* (2 Corinthians 12:1–7).

As seers and seeing people, we need to walk according to the legalities of heaven. We are not to boast about our encounters but walk in the humility of Christ who dwells in heaven. We are not always to share what we see or learn in heaven but must look to the Lord who called us upward for permission on what and when to share. To do otherwise is to grieve the Holy Spirit of God. While God may choose to take you to heaven just to train your eyes or bless your soul, repeated heavenly encounters without bringing back the fruit of heaven are questionable.

We could share many legitimate heavenly exposures and encounters in this book from reputable seers and others who have had legitimate experiences and come back with profound revelation, messages, and knowledge that blessed the Body of Christ. However, we believe Jones's encounter was one of the most significant—complete with teachable moments about how to handle heavenly encounters and revelations—and is especially appropriate for the times we are in as a Body of Christ.

In 2016, Jones told the story of a dramatic encounter with heaven that left him with a message that impacts a generation. As you read it, notice how it is biblical—meaning it is in line with the Bible and the ways of God—as all authentic encounters are. Notice also how Jones asks questions to learn and take away the information God wants him to understand and convey.

Did You Learn to Love?

Here is a transcript of Jones's vision:

> I was in pain on the earth and blood was shooting out of my mouth like a geyser.
>
> And all of a sudden I wasn't in pain anymore. This Man, the Parakleet stood by my side, the Holy Spirit, we started walking. And as we walked, I saw a Man who was white light. All white light was around Him, but He was the whitest of all white lights. He had His hands out. As I came into that white light, there came a feeling over me like I had never known before. I asked the Man beside me, "What is that?"
>
> The Man (Holy Spirit) said, "It is the love of God." I said, "It's just so wonderful, it's so glorious." And He said, "That's what it is, it's the glory of God." I said, "How can it be both?" It's in John 17. The love I had with the Father, the glory I had with the Father. So that was the greatest experience I have ever had. Just enveloped in His glorious love. That's possible down here. The glory of God is coming and it is going to be in His glorious love.
>
> I noticed another group of people on my left side and they had like a conveyor belt underneath them. And they were wrapped up in all different kinds of things. And I looked at them and I asked this Man, "Why are they wrapped up that way?" And He said, "They were wrapped up in the

earth with their gods. It's the gods they worshipped on the earth, that followed them into death. They were on their way to Hell with their gods. I saw a man wrapped up in dollar bills. I saw a man wrapped up in his sod or grass; his yard was his god. I saw a man that had no body, he was just one big head. He was an atheist, he worshipped himself; he was his own god and going to Hell with it.

I saw all manner of things who people worshipped on the earth; who they are going to spend eternity with. Well, I worshipped the Lord and I am going to spend eternity with Him. But these others that don't are going to spend eternity in total darkness with their god. And their gods will be their tormentors, not a hundred thousand years, but eternity.

So I looked at that line. It was so horrible, and everyone when they came there, they recognized Him. Their eyes got big, and everyone that is going to Hell has had a witness in one way or another that there is a God. And every one of them willingly denied Him. For each two in the line that I was in, there was ninety-eight in the other line.

I watched the Lord speak to people that were coming there. And He asked them only one question: "Did you learn to love?" He's not going to ask you what you did. If you learn to love you are going to do that which is right. Did you learn to love? He would ask them that question and they would say, "Yes Lord," and He would kiss them right on the lips and embrace them and the double doors of His heart would open and they would go right on in.

Some of them had a lot of angels with them and they would go on in. The angels went in because they had testimonies;

they helped people do things on the earth. They have no testimony until they help you do something. You are the ones that will judge angels by their rewards for what they helped you do. They are more willing to help you do something, than you are willing to submit and let them help you do it.

As I came close to the Lord, I was thinking, "I learned to love. I'm OK, I'm going home." As I did, He held His hand up to me and said, "No I want you to go back." I told Him, "It was too hard to get here. I don't want to because I wasn't doing any good there." He said, "You are a liar, because you spoke My Words and My Words will always bring it to pass." I said, "Well nobody was believing it and it was painful." He said, "Yes, and you have a cowardly nature too. [Up there, it's the truth.] But you love. You had a heart for souls. I want you to go back. If you look at that line over there and then tell me you want to come in, I will bring you in."

I looked at that line and looked at their faces and said I would go back for one. I would go back and spend a day on a cross for one. He said, "I'm not sending you back for that. I'm sending you back to wake up the Church because I am going to bring a billion youth to Myself. In one of the greatest waves of all times. I'm going to honor Myself beyond anything that man can imagine. I want you to go back and touch the Church and speak to the Church of what I am going to do in these last days." So I told Him I would come back.

I came back. I thought that when I come back into my body I would be healed. As I came back I saw two of the biggest angels I have ever seen. I know who they are. They are the resurrection angels. And I saw the death spirit and he left when I came back in. And when I went back into the body I wasn't healed. The pain was there and I couldn't understand why. And I was gone probably for about three hours. The pain was there and I said, "What's going on Lord?" And then I heard a phone ring. And I saw people answering the phone and they were saying, "Bob Jones needs prayer." And they would start praying and I felt better. And it was a Friday.

People kept praying and it kept increasing and increasing. And then people came over and prayed for me Friday night 'till the pain wasn't hardly there. And then Friday night, Saturday morning at three o'clock the last person quit praying for me. I could see who was praying for me. The pain was coming back and I thought, "Boy it's going to be a long time."

And then I saw an old sister who wasn't thought highly of in the church because she didn't take too many baths. She always sat in the last seat in back. And she cleaned offices for a living. She got up early in the morning and cleaned offices. And her phone rang and she answered it. She got up at three o'clock in the morning and started praying for me and I went to sleep. And then she had to go to work at five, and others began to pray for me, so Saturday was pretty good. It went pretty well. People came over Saturday and I thought, "Well I know He sent me back down here to live." And prayer and intercession sure made the difference.

And Saturday night it went on pretty good until about three o'clock and all the other prayer ended. Except hers. She got up and went to praying for me again. She prayed for me until about seven o'clock. She didn't have to work on a Sunday. At seven o'clock was the worst time that I saw because there was no prayer. People were going to church.

And it was really bad until about 10:05. At ten o'clock, Viola asked me, "How are you doing?" I told her I was worse than I had ever been and I was swelling so bad I couldn't even get out of bed. At 10:05 I became totally normal, totally delivered. I got up and we went to church and I testified of it.

I found out the value of prayer. And I found out the value of not having an opinion about saints. I found out the value of ministry. That one saint was able to void all of it to where I could sleep.[3]

Can We Really Enter the Heavenly Realm Now?

So how can you enter the heavenly realm? We don't believe you can choose to have dramatic encounters in the heaven any more than you can choose to have a dream from God. The Holy Spirit invites us into seer realms through Jesus, who is the door (see John 10:7). Technically, if we are born again, we walk in a duality. We are simultaneously walking in the earth realm and seated in the heavenly realm. Consider the Holy Spirit–inspired words of Paul the apostle in Ephesians 2:4–7:

> *But God, who is rich in mercy, because of His great love with which He loved us, even when we were dead in trespasses, made us alive together with Christ (by grace you have been saved), and raised us up together, and made us sit together in the heavenly places in Christ Jesus, that in the ages to come He might show the exceeding riches of His grace in His kindness toward us in Christ Jesus.*

God has made us sit together in heavenly places in Christ. This is our legal position. It's the position from which we war. It's the position from which we see in the spirit. This is not our practical everyday living condition in the earth realm where we witness death and destruction, sickness and disease, pain and sorrow. But it is our legal position. Is it so strange to think we could, by God's invitation, enter into the heavenly realm?

The Amplified Bible, Classic Edition translation of Ephesians 2:6 goes a little deeper: *"He raised us up together with Him and made us sit down together [giving us joint seating with Him] in the heavenly sphere [by virtue of our being] in Christ Jesus (the Messiah, the Anointed One)."*

The Passion Translation of Ephesians 2:6 really drives home this reality: *"He raised us up with Christ the exalted One, and we ascended with him into the glorious perfection and authority of the heavenly realm, for we are now co-seated as one with Christ!"*

If you are in Christ—and you are, as Scriptures repeatedly refer to us as in Christ—then you are legally seated in heavenly places. You have some right and invitation, by default, to take your seat. That said, I don't believe we ascend and descend to heaven at will. But I do believe there is a legal right to enter the seer realm through dreams and visions and the opportunity to ascend as God wills. Given all the books and dramatic recounts, it seems God wills more than we understand or have faith for.

How to Enter the Heavenly Realm

So how do we enter the heavenly realm? The first step is understanding that heaven exists as a city where God is enthroned. It's closer than we think. It is not on the other side of Pluto. There's actually a thin veil between the seen and unseen realm. God invites people at times into this realm—or sometimes brings them there without any forewarning. Either way, you can begin to position your heart for a heavenly invitation in several ways.

Study heaven in the Bible.

If you want to position yourself to see heaven, whether in a dream, a vision, or an actual encounter, study what the Bible says about heaven. Get familiar with the landscape and language of heaven. Get rooted and grounded in the Word so that you avoid false encounters with angels of light. Demonstrate your interest in this eternal city by studying to show yourself approved (see 2 Tim. 2:5).

Read books on heavenly encounters.

Reading books on heavenly encounters can stir your faith. We know there is much more to be said and experienced about heaven than what the Bible divulges. Of course, we need to be careful to read books by reputable authors who are grounded in the Word and have a relationship with the Spirit so a spirit of error doesn't fool us. Don't just read any book because you can receive impartations from what you read just as you can from the laying on of hands.

Imagine yourself at the throne.

Imagine yourself in the pages of the Bible and what it says about heaven. Picture the sea of glass. Imagine yourself at the gates. See the river of life or standing at the throne. God gave you an imagination. You can use it for holy purposes. We don't have to let the New Age movement steal the realm of imagination.

According to *Merriam-Webster*'s dictionary, *imagination* is "the act or power of forming a mental image of something not present to the senses or never before wholly perceived in reality."[4] You can choose to picture Bible scenes. It is one way we meditate on the Word of God. When you use your imagination to see yourself in heaven, you are essentially walking in Philippians 4:8: *"Finally, brethren, whatever things are true, whatever things are noble, whatever things are just, whatever things are pure, whatever things are lovely, whatever things are of good report, if there is any virtue and if there is anything praiseworthy—meditate on these things."*

Get in the Spirit.

Get into Spirit. Remember, John the Revelator was *"in the Spirit on the Lord's Day"* (Rev. 1:10). Worship can open the heavens over your life and elicit an invitation. Prayer can bring you into the spirit. Praise can bring you into the spirit. Reading the Word can bring you into the spirit.

Meditate on your position in Christ.

We'll go in-depth on meditation in a later chapter, but this is worth mentioning now. Meditate on your position in Christ. That means finding and reading—and reading again and again—every Scripture that talks about who you are "in Christ" or "in Him" or "to whom" or "through Christ" or "by Christ," and so on—and what that affords you. Here are a few to get you started: John 15:5; Acts 17:28; 1 Corinthians 1:30; 2 Corinthians 5:21; Colossians 1:13–14; and Colossians 1:26–27.

We'll end this chapter with a quote from Patricia King: "Do you know it's absolutely the portion of every single believer in Jesus to have access into heaven, to have encounter in heaven, to have experiences with God in heaven and that is before you die. That is while you are still living and breathing in the earth."

CHAPTER 8

THE DEMONIC DIMENSION

The demonic realm is raging in the unseen world. If demons weren't active in the seer realm, John the Beloved would not have warned us to test the spirits, to see if they are from God (see 1 John 4:1). While we'd all rather see angels or heaven, the demonic realm is part and parcel of the seer's visual landscape, and God can choose to open it at any time.

When Jesus walked the earth, He confronted the demonic realm time and time again. Indeed, He cast out demons everywhere He went. In Acts 10:38 Luke chronicled how Jesus went about doing good and healing all who were oppressed by the devil. The Bible gives believers glimpses into the demonic realm—but seers and seeing people sometimes see into this realm with their spiritual eyes.

Jesus describes the moment He saw satan fall from heaven like lightning (see Luke 10:18). I imagine He also saw one-third of the angels who followed Lucifer in his insurrection fall. What a sight! I also imagine Jesus saw the spirit of infirmity, the spirit of epilepsy, the spirit of fear, and other spirits that were plaguing the captives He set free. What a sight the man with the legion of demons must have been!

With regards to the demonic realm, the seer gift works strongly with the gift of discerning of spirits. While discernment should work to discern the Holy Spirit and angels as well as demon powers, some seers and seeing people are more bent to see into the demonic realm than others. Regardless of a seer's particular bent or assignment in the Body of Christ, seers and seeing people are quick to discern when satan is transforming himself as an angel of light (see 2 Cor. 11:14).

A Vivid Picture of a War in Heaven

Before we move deeper into the demonic realm, let's take a moment to understand that satan does have a kingdom. It's called the kingdom of darkness (see Col. 1:13). The Bible calls satan the *"god of this world"* (see 2 Cor. 4:4 NASB).

Satan's kingdom is highly organized in a military-like hierarchy of principalities, powers, rulers of darkness, and spiritual wickedness outlined in Ephesians 6:12. I like the Amplified Bible, Classic Edition of this verse because it draws it out:

> *For we are not wrestling with flesh and blood [contending only with physical opponents], but against the despotisms, against the powers, against [the master spirits who are] the world rulers of this present darkness, against the spirit forces of wickedness in the heavenly (supernatural) sphere.*

Colossians 1:16 offers even more insight into this hierarchy:

> *For it was in Him that all things were created, in heaven and on earth, things seen and things unseen, whether thrones, dominions, rulers, or authorities; all things were*

created and exist through Him [by His service, intervention] and in and for Him (NASB).

As a seer or seeing person, you'll find the imagery around the fall of satan fascinating. Try to picture this as you read it in Revelation 12:7–12:

> *Then war broke out in heaven; Michael and his angels went forth to battle with the dragon, and the dragon and his angels fought.*
>
> *But they were defeated, and there was no room found for them in heaven any longer.*
>
> *And the huge dragon was cast down and out—that age-old serpent, who is called the Devil and Satan, he who is the seducer (deceiver) of all humanity the world over; he was forced out and down to the earth, and his angels were flung out along with him.*
>
> *Then I heard a strong (loud) voice in heaven, saying, Now it has come—the salvation and the power and the kingdom (the dominion, the reign) of our God, and the power (the sovereignty, the authority) of His Christ (the Messiah); for the accuser of our brethren, he who keeps bringing before our God charges against them day and night, has been cast out!*
>
> *And they have overcome (conquered) him by means of the blood of the Lamb and by the utterance of their testimony, for they did not love and cling to life even when faced with death [holding their lives cheap till they had to die for their witnessing].*
>
> *Therefore be glad (exult), O heavens and you that dwell in them! But woe to you, O earth and sea, for the devil has come down to you in fierce anger (fury), because he knows that he has [only] a short time [left]!* (AMPC)

Yes, the demonic realm is real and raging. The enemy comes to kill, steal, and destroy, according to Jesus' words in John 10:10. The enemy roams about like a roaring lion seeking someone to devour, according to 1 Peter 5:8. We're in a wrestling match with demons, according to Ephesians 6:12.

Seers and seeing people are positioned to see what the enemy is doing in the spirit realm—and as with everything the Lord shows us, there is a purpose for the seeing. God could be calling you to make intercession over someone's life or over a church, city, or nation to push back the darkness that's working to defy His will. He could be calling you to take it a step further—to sound the alarm to warn and mobilize a greater intercessory prayer shield. The Lord could also be showing you someone's need for deliverance.

Make no mistake, He's not showing you to scare you—and you should not be scared by what you see in the demonic realm. You have authority over unclean spirits, to cast them out. You have authority over demon powers, to bind them. You have authority over all the power of the enemy, and nothing shall by any means harm you (see Luke 10:19). Know this: if there was a war in heaven—and there was—there will be wars on earth. It is your privilege as a seer or seeing person to uncover the enemy's plans and combat them.

Daniel's Vision of the Demonic Realm

Daniel had dramatic visions from the Lord. One of them is found in chapter 7 of the book he chronicled. Pay close attention to these verses, and you will find the balance in seeing into the demonic realm. We're reading a long passage from Daniel 7:1–14:

> *In the first year of Belshazzar king of Babylon, Daniel had a dream and visions of his head while on his bed. Then he wrote down the dream, telling the main facts.*

Daniel spoke, saying, "I saw in my vision by night, and behold, the four winds of heaven were stirring up the Great Sea. And four great beasts came up from the sea, each different from the other. The first was like a lion, and had eagle's wings. I watched till its wings were plucked off; and it was lifted up from the earth and made to stand on two feet like a man, and a man's heart was given to it. And suddenly another beast, a second, like a bear. It was raised up on one side, and had three ribs in its mouth between its teeth. And they said thus to it: 'Arise, devour much flesh!'

"After this I looked, and there was another, like a leopard, which had on its back four wings of a bird. The beast also had four heads, and dominion was given to it.

"After this I saw in the night visions, and behold, a fourth beast, dreadful and terrible, exceedingly strong. It had huge iron teeth; it was devouring, breaking in pieces, and trampling the residue with its feet. It was different from all the beasts that were before it, and it had ten horns. I was considering the horns, and there was another horn, a little one, coming up among them, before whom three of the first horns were plucked out by the roots. And there, in this horn, were eyes like the eyes of a man, and a mouth speaking pompous words.

"I watched till thrones were put in place, and the Ancient of Days was seated; His garment was white as snow, and the hair of His head was like pure wool. His throne was a fiery flame, its wheels a burning fire; a fiery stream issued and came forth from before Him. A thousand thousands ministered to Him; ten thousand times ten thousand stood before Him. The court was seated, and the books were opened.

"I watched then because of the sound of the pompous words which the horn was speaking; I watched till the beast was slain, and its body destroyed and given to the burning flame. As for the rest of the beasts, they had their dominion taken away, yet their lives were prolonged for a season and a time.

"I was watching in the night visions, and behold, One like the Son of Man, coming with the clouds of heaven! He came to the Ancient of Days, and they brought Him near before Him. Then to Him was given dominion and glory and a kingdom, that all peoples, nations, and languages should serve Him. His dominion is an everlasting dominion, which shall not pass away, and His kingdom the one which shall not be destroyed."

Navigating Visions of the Demonic

Now, notice this. Daniel was seeing a demonic assignment. Daniel 7:21–22 reveals, *"I was watching; and the same horn was making war against the saints, and prevailing against them, until the Ancient of Days came, and a judgment was made in favor of the saints of the Most High, and the time came for the saints to possess the kingdom."*

Daniel saw the demonic assignment, but Daniel did not stop looking until he saw the Lord and His will in the spirit realm. This is where many seers and seeing people fall short. They see what is going on in the spirit realm on the dark side, but they either become afraid or overwhelmed and don't keep looking, as Daniel did, for the Lord so they can get a strategy or bring a message of hope.

As I described in my book *Angels on Assignment Again*, a friend of mine talked me into hiking up into the Smoky Mountains in North Carolina. She claimed the journey was only a mile but it took every minute of daylight, right up until dusk.

When we finally arrived to the "peaceful secluded area where God dwelled" as she claimed, I was hungry, sore, tired, freezing, scared, and cold when the sun set. When utter darkness fell, I closed the tent's zipper and lay my head on the tiny pillow. There was not a star in the sky, and the moon was missing. The only light I could see emanated from the fire's flickering flames. It felt as if we had descended into hell.

Determined to make the best of it, I bundled myself up as tightly as I could and started counting sheep in my head to take my mind off the bears. The only problem was I heard a bear outside the tent prowling around. I am not sure why, but I unzipped the tent door and poked my head outside. I don't know what I thought I would do if I saw a bear there.

What I saw was something blacker than black lunge toward me with vicious force. It scared me half to death and I screamed. My body flew to the back of the tent. Then I froze. Speechless. Finally, I managed to utter one word: "Bear..."

My friend did not believe me. She decided to take a look for herself. I feared for her life but was still frozen like an ice sculpture, so I watched in silent terror as she looked out the tent doors. I was sure she had sealed her fate.

She stuck her head out for what seemed like an eternity when suddenly I heard her exclaim, "Wow! Wow! Wow!"

Somewhat annoyed, I said, "What?"

Her only response, "Wow."

Especially annoyed at this point, I replied, "What?!"

She then informed me that there were giant angels, one on either side of the tent, with swords drawn. They were protecting us. They were angels of protection. God opened her eyes and allowed her to see in the spirit realm. What I had seen, I later learned, was a spirit of fear. I felt like

I got the short end of that supernatural stick. After all, it was her fault we needed angelic protection from bears and fear demons in the first place!

Encountering the Realm Called Hell

Beyond the demonic realm is hell. Many seers and seeing people have visited hell or looked into this realm. A good number of books have resulted from these horrifying encounters. Unlike the demonic realm, it's normal to be shaken to the core by these encounters. I have never encountered hell nor do I ever want to. I have heard stories of people being out of commission for days and even weeks after such visitations.

In her book *The Hell Conspiracy* my good friend Laurie Ditto from the International House of Prayer in Kansas City, tells about a vision in which Jesus took her to hell. I have heard her tell the story firsthand, and it still shakes her. I've seen her go through six bottles of water while shaking, sweating and crying at the memory.

Ditto companies the visitation as a terrible, life-changing accident. The details of what she calls the worst day of her entire life and possibly the most life-giving day of her existence are still etched in her memory. The Lord initiated this encounter during the weekly two-hour evangelism staff meeting at IHOPKC. The meeting began with worship, and she was standing in the back room, lifting up her hands and engaging her mind with the risen King.

As she recalls, the worship leader was leading the evangelists into prayer for their lost family members, friends, neighbors, and coworkers.

> "As we sang an evangelistic song, I felt the presence of
> holiness come into the room. The song gripped me and
> just seemed to add to the excitement I already felt," Ditto
> recalls. "The music was captivating and took me to what I
> will call a worship place....The feeling in the room was the
> same as other times that I had been invited to come away

with the Lord to visit Heaven. I knew I was being invited to go in the spirit. The holiness had come for me. I said, 'Yes.'"

Suddenly, she explains, the front of the room opened up. When she opened her eyes she saw hell unlocked. She heard what she describes as massive gates creak open and felt the fire of hell enter the room. When she looked with her eyes wide open she saw hell through the gates:

> "I saw it! I was shocked that it was right there. Wasn't it supposed to be in the center of the earth or below us? To say I panicked is an understatement!"

Everyone else continued in prayer and worship, unaware of what Ditto was seeing or experiencing. No one else was encountering this horrific sight. Ditto watched as the gates of hell opened and the people around her were worshipping at the same time.

> "I frantically looked to see who might help me. The others didn't see the gates, hear that sound, or feel the heat. Instinctively, I started screaming," Ditto recalls. "I felt the sound of fear coming from my own body. I knew that my spirit was being demanded to submit. As I screamed, my spirit was also making a sound that deeply hurt my heart and brain while it also panicked every blood cell in my body.
>
> "Something came flying past the gates of Hell. It was coming for me. It was like an arm without fingers that grabbed me and sucked me into Hell. The arm was very powerful. It was attached to me like a suction cup in the area of my chest and began dragging me further into Hell. As quickly as it shot out from Hell, it just as quickly moved back. I

tried to pull back and break the hold it had on me but it was too powerful.

"Before I could blink, I knew this—it was too late. The gates slammed shut with a terrible sound of finality. I knew there was no man on this side or that who could ever open those gates. Only Jesus could because He owns Hell....I passed through gates that trapped the darkness inside. The first thing I knew when I got there: I was in Hell.... The realization that I was in Hell was unquestionably shocking and beyond hurtful! I don't know how to explain just how panicked I was, although you may understand a bit if you've ever been lost."[1]

Hell Is Painfully Real

Hell is real, just like heaven is real. We do have some images of hell from the pages of Scripture. We know hell is a place of sorrow (see 2 Sam. 22:6). Hell is a place of utter darkness (see 2 Pet. 2:17). Hell is a place of eternal destruction (see 2 Thess. 1:9). Hell is a place with no rest day or night (see Rev. 14:11). Hell is a place of suffering in a lake of burning sulfur (see Rev. 19:20). Hell is a place where inhabitants are eternally separated from God, and that is ultimately what makes it so horrifying.

If you see into the realm of hell, as Ditto and many others have, you are likely to have the imagery burned on your soul forever. You will be shaken by images of death, sorrow, pain, and destruction. If you enter the hell realm, you will feel fear. You will feel the separation from God. Clearly, this is not something we want to see, but God can choose to open our eyes to this realm for His purposes. His purposes, in these cases, is usually tied to evangelism and a love for the lost—for intercession.

Jesus spoke of hell more than anyone else in Scripture. In fact, He spoke of hell more than He spoke of Heaven. He called it a place of eternal punishment (see Matt. 25:46). He said there is fire in hell (see Matt. 5:22). He said hell has gates (see Matt. 16:18). He said there is weeping and gnashing of teeth in hell, which is outer darkness (see Matt. 8:12). He said hell is a place where worms prey on dead bodies and fire is never quenched (see Mark 9:44). He said hell is a place of torment (see Luke 16:23). He said this fire is everlasting (see Matt. 18:8).

If you see into the realm of hell, you will find it just as Jesus described it. You will see, as Ditto did, the gates of hell. You will see the torment and darkness. You will see fire. You may even feel, as Ditto did, the fire of hell. While in hell, Ditto says she knew and felt many things all at once. She describes four distinct pains. The first was for water. Immediately, she explains, all the water left her body creating a desperate painful thirst. We see a parallel to Ditto's visit to hell in Scripture. Luke 16:19–25:

> *There was a certain rich man who was clothed in purple and fine linen and fared sumptuously every day. But there was a certain beggar named Lazarus, full of sores, who was laid at his gate, desiring to be fed with the crumbs which fell from the rich man's table. Moreover the dogs came and licked his sores. So it was that the beggar died, and was carried by the angels to Abraham's bosom. The rich man also died and was buried. And being in torments in Hades, he lifted up his eyes and saw Abraham afar off, and Lazarus in his bosom. Then he cried and said, "Father Abraham, have mercy on me, and send Lazarus that he may dip the tip of his finger in water and cool my tongue; for I am tormented in this flame."*

Ditto also noticed her bones turned black, and the first breath in hell allowed fire to touch everything in her. She agreed with the judgment of hell and her views on unforgiveness taking people to hell changed.

> In Hell I already knew the complete truth from God's perspective. The ways of God are righteous, always righteous!

Even though I wished it were not so, I knew that it was. The judgment of God is true. Everyone knows that truth there. The judgment of me being in Hell eternally for not forgiving people on the earth was completely righteous. In my own knowledge, being in Hell was completely righteous. I can't tell you what that did to me then, or the soberness that it puts in me even today. It's not like on the earth where innocent people have gone to jail for something they didn't do. That never happens in Hell. Everyone in Hell is there because they are guilty. Because they would not love and obey God.

As I faced the reality of my judgment, I was in overload. I was inundated with an ever-increasing fear and knowledge that Hell is not only everything that I had read in the Bible but so much worse. But there is no overload shut-down mechanism in Hell. No shutting off, no taking a break, no passing out, and no quitting. The horribleness and pain in Hell accelerated and continued to get worse. I was literally experiencing inside my body the truth I had read in the Bible....At the end of the vision, I reentered the earthly realm yelling. The worship was still going on, but I took center stage from the back of the room with my screaming.[2]

Thank God, our citizenship is in heaven. If you see into the realm of hell, get prayer support. It will mark you forever. Don't ask to enter this realm. And if you find yourself there, when you come out of the encounter, write out every detail and start preaching the gospel. You will be one of the relative few in history who the Lord shows this realm.

CHAPTER 9

THE ECSTATIC DIMENSION

Trances are mysterious. We don't read much about them in the Bible, and, unlike prophecy, we don't have much to look toward in the modern church. You can't be trained to go into a trance. You can't choose to go into a God-ordained trance. You can't choose to come out of a trance. Trances are somewhat of an enigma—and they are also part of the seer realm.

More specifically, trances are part of the ecstatic realm of the spirit. The ecstatic realm is a realm marked by ecstasy. We have relegated that word to a feeling of the flesh—there's even a hallucinogenic drug by this name—but ecstasy is actually a biblical concept. It's one of many mystical aspects of the prophetic.

To understand the ecstatic realm, you have to understand mystics, which is just another word for *mysteries*. *Merriam-Webster*'s dictionary defines *mystical* as "having a spiritual meaning or reality that is neither apparent to the senses nor obvious to the intelligence."[1] Although some high-profile Christians have given a bad name to mystics, Christian mystics of over one thousand years ago were men and women of great revelation who left behind understandings into the mysteries of God and His Word like this:

> Truly it is a trustworthy word and deserving of every welcome, your almighty Word, Lord, which in such deep silence made its way down from the Father's royal throne and speaks to us better by its silence. Hear what this loving and mysterious silence of the eternal Word speaks to us. He speaks peace for the holy people upon whom reverence for him and his example impose a religious silence. —Guerric of Igny, an eleventh century Cistercian abbot

Mysteries Tied to the Seer Realm

Paul, who wrote two-thirds of the New Testament by direct revelation, spoke of mystic concepts again and again the Bible. If we are rooted and grounded in the Bible in the mystic realm, including trances, being caught up in the spirit and transported in the spirit, we can engage with the whole counsel of God and understand better the mysteries of the Kingdom.

Mysteries are tied to the seer realm—and the Bible speaks of them over and over again. Although this short chapter is not intended to give a deep explanation of the mystic realm, it's important that you understand some fundamentals as they relate to the seer realm. God makes mysteries known to us by revelation. Paul explains it this way:

> *If indeed you have heard of the dispensation of the grace of God which was given to me for you, how that by revelation He made known to me the mystery (as I have briefly written already, by which, when you read, you may understand my knowledge in the mystery of Christ), which in other ages was not made known to the sons of men, as it has now been revealed by the Spirit to His holy apostles and prophets:*

that the Gentiles should be fellow heirs, of the same body, and partakers of His promise in Christ through the gospel (Ephesians 3:2–6).

Mystery in that verse comes from the Greek word *musterion*. According to the King James Version New Testament Greek lexicon, it means, "hidden thing, secret, mystery; generally mysteries, religious secrets, confided only to the initiated and not to ordinary mortals; a hidden or secret thing, not obvious to the understanding; a hidden purpose or counsel; the secret counsels which govern God in dealing with the righteous, which are hidden from ungodly and wicked men but plain to the godly; in rabbinic writings, it denotes the mystic or hidden sense, of an OT saying; of an image or form seen in a vision; of a dream."[2]

Vine's Expository Dictionary says *musterion* "denotes, not the mysterious (as with the Eng. word), but that which, being outside the range of unassisted natural apprehension, can be made known only by divine revelation, and is made known in a manner and at a time appointed by God, and to those only who are illuminated by His Spirit."[3]

You can see how mysteries are tied to the prophetic realm because Amos 3:7 tells us, *"Surely the Lord God does nothing, unless He reveals His secret to His servants the prophets."* And you can see a clear tie in to the seer realm through images, visions, and dreams. Treasures of wisdom and knowledge are hidden in the mystic realm. Consider Paul's words in Colossians 2:1–3:

> *For I want you to know what a great conflict I have for you and those in Laodicea, and for as many as have not seen my face in the flesh, that their hearts may be encouraged, being knit together in love, and attaining to all riches of the full assurance of understanding, to the knowledge of the mystery of God, both of the Father and of Christ, in whom are hidden all the treasures of wisdom and knowledge.*

The Holy Spirit Reveals

The Holy Spirit is the revealer. He is the one who revealed Christ to our heart and convicted us, drawing us to our Savior. That was just the beginning. The Holy Spirit wants us to come to the knowledge of the mystery of God, which unlocks treasures, wisdom, and knowledge. Sometimes he reveals mysteries through His Word, sometimes through a still, small voice, and sometimes through the seer realm.

After speaking in parables, Jesus said to His disciples, *"Because it has been given to you to know the mysteries of the kingdom of heaven, but to them it has not been given"* (Matt. 13:11). This word *mystery* appears in the New Testament twenty-six times and speaks of:

- The mystery of Gentiles being grafted into the vine (see Rom. 11:24–25)
- The wisdom of God in a mystery (see 1 Cor. 2:7)
- The resurrection of believers is a mystery (see 1 Cor. 15:51)
- His being made known to us the mystery of His will (see Eph. 1:9)
- There's the mystery of the gospel (see Eph. 6:19)
- There's the mystery of Christ (see Col. 4:3)
- There's the mystery of iniquity (see 2 Thess. 2:7)
- There's the mystery of faith (see 1 Tim. 3:9)
- There's the mystery of godliness (see 1 Tim. 3:16)
- There's the mystery of the seven stars (see Rev. 1:20)

Unlocking Mysteries of God by Faith

Jesus wants His disciples to know the mysteries of the kingdom of heaven. We have to press into the mystical and ecstatic realms. These realms are largely misunderstood, and error can creep in if we are not rooted in the Word. But the reality is the Word has plenty to say about this dimension.

The Bible calls us stewards of the mysteries of God (see 1 Cor. 4:1). We can't steward something we haven't unlocked. Mysteries become revelation as God opens the eyes of our heart so we can see what we could not see before.

Proverbs 25:2 reveals: *"It is the glory of God to conceal a matter, but the glory of kings is to search out a matter."* And Deuteronomy 29:29 says, *"The secret things belong to the Lord our God, but those things which are revealed belong to us and to our children forever, that we may do all the words of this law."* Jeremiah 33:3 instructs us: *"Call to Me, and I will answer you, and show you great and mighty things, which you do not know."*

There are mysteries, like salvation, into which the angels long to look (see 1 Pet. 1:12). The purpose of mysteries revealed is to release faith to obey what the Lord is calling us to do. This is not for knowledge sake alone. *"Knowledge puffs up"* (1 Cor. 8:1). Consider this quote:

> I pray you: seek more to embody God than to merely have knowledge of God. For knowledge can deceive us with pride, but a meek, loving awareness will not deceive. Knowledge puffs up, but love builds up (1 Corinthians 8:1). Knowledge leads to travail, whereas awareness leads to rest.[4]

In closing, we'll take you into some of the more mysterious aspects of the seer realm so that you have a foundation to keep you securely tied to the Word of God in an age where deception is running rampant.

CHAPTER 10

THE TRANCE DIMENSION

Trances are not merely the domain of shamans, New Agers, and DJs with pumping beats. A trance is not hypnosis, although hypnotized people do experience a trancelike state. Trances are not relegated to the realm of witches and warlocks, though these dark agents do use trances to enter into astral projection, a counterfeit of the biblical concept of being transported in the Spirit.

The enemy always works to counterfeit what God is doing, and because of this many have feared to even learn of the trance realm. The reality is trances are biblical, and we need to understand what the Bible says about them. What is a trance? Before we go any further, it's helpful to see various definitions that will lay a foundation for your faith.

Noah Webster's 1828 Dictionary defines trance this way, "An ecstasy; a state in which the soul seems to have passed out of the body into celestial regions, or to be rapt into visions."[1] A trance is a state of one who is "out of himself," according to *Easton's Bible Dictionary*.[2] The word *trance* comes from the Greek word *ekstasis*, form which the word *ecstasy* is derived.

According to *The King James New Testament Greek Lexicon*, *ekstatis* means "a throwing of the mind out of its normal state, alienation of mind, whether such as makes a lunatic or that of a man who by some sudden emotion is transported as it were out of himself, so that in this rapt condition, although he is awake, his mind is drawn off from all surrounding objects and wholly fixed on things divine that he sees nothing but the forms and images lying within, and thinks that he perceives with his bodily eyes and ears realities shown him by God."[3]

I suppose it's hard to describe it if you've not experienced it, but *Smith's Bible Dictionary* goes a little deeper, saying a trance is: "The... state in which a man has passed out of the usual order of his life, beyond the usual limits of consciousness and volition, being rapt in causes of this state are to be traced commonly to strong religious impressions. Whatever explanation may be given of it, it is true of many, if not of most, of those who have left the stamp of their own character on the religious history of mankind, that they have been liable to pass at times into this abnormal state."[4]

The *International Bible Encyclopedia* defines trance this way: "The condition expressed by this word is a mental state in which the person affected is partially or wholly unconscious of objective sensations, but intensely alive to subjective impressions which, however they may be originated, are felt as if they were revelations from without. They may take the form of visual or auditory sensations or else of impressions of taste, smell, heat or cold, and sometimes these conditions precede epileptic seizures constituting what is named the aura epileptica."[5]

What the Bible Says About Trances

We only see trances mentioned five times in the Bible, but that is more than enough to set a principle of a way God moves on us and speaks to us. By the mouth of two or three witnesses every word is established (see Deut. 19:15). We'll start with the Old Testament, where we see two mentions of trances and then move to the New Testament, where we see trances mentioned three times.

Balaam's trance

Balaam, the false prophet who a king tried to hire to curse Israel, went into a trance. We read about that in Numbers 24:1–4:

> *And when Balaam saw that it pleased the Lord to bless Israel, he went not, as at other times, to seek for enchantments, but he set his face toward the wilderness. And Balaam lifted up his eyes, and he saw Israel abiding in his tents according to their tribes; and the spirit of God came upon him.*
>
> *And he took up his parable, and said, Balaam the son of Beor hath said, and the man whose eyes are open hath said: He hath said, which heard the words of God, which saw the vision of the Almighty, falling into a trance, but having his eyes open* (KJV).

Notice when he fell into this trance, his eyes were open. He was not asleep, but it seemed he was in a sleeplike state, not moving.

Peter's trance

Peter fell into a trance that opened his eyes to preach the Gospel to the Gentiles. Let's look at the entire account in Acts 10:10–17:

> *Then he became very hungry and wanted to eat; but while they made ready, he fell into a trance and saw heaven opened and an object like a great sheet bound at the four corners, descending to him and let down to the earth. In it were all kinds of four-footed animals of the earth, wild beasts, creeping things, and birds of the air. And a voice came to him, "Rise, Peter; kill and eat."*
>
> *But Peter said, "Not so, Lord! For I have never eaten anything common or unclean."*

And a voice spoke to him again the second time, "What God has cleansed you must not call common." This was done three times. And the object was taken up into heaven again.

Now while Peter wondered within himself what this vision which he had seen meant, behold, the men who had been sent from Cornelius had made inquiry for Simon's house, and stood before the gate.

Notice, Peter saw a vision in the trance. Many people who fall into trances report having seen visions. Some others can't even describe what they have seen or didn't see anything.

Paul's trance

Paul fell into a trance in Acts 22:17–21 in which the Lord gave him a warning and a commission to preach the Gospel to the Gentiles.

I was in a trance and saw Him saying to me, "Make haste and get out of Jerusalem quickly, for they will not receive your testimony concerning Me." So I said, "Lord, they know that in every synagogue I imprisoned and beat those who believe on You. And when the blood of Your martyr Stephen was shed, I also was standing by consenting to his death, and guarding the clothes of those who were killing him." Then He said to me, "Depart, for I will send you far from here to the Gentiles."

Notice, that Paul got instruction in the trance, just as Peter did. Trances, like any other supernatural encounter, are purposeful.

What Happens in Trances?

I've never fallen into a trance, but I know people who have—and it's totally biblical. We only see people falling into trances a few times in the Bible, but there is enough evidence from the Word of God and from modern expressions to back up this scriptural supernatural experience.

Maria Woodworth-Etter, a powerful voice from the late 1800s and early 1900s who was moving in the supernatural before Asuza Street or the Charismatic movement made its mark on church history, was known for trances.

Indeed, Woodworth-Etter was a Pentecostal forerunner. She saw great outpourings of God's Spirit in the Midwest before entering the West Coast to win souls for God. In Oakland, California, she bought an eight thousand-seat tent in 1889 and packed it out with people hungry to watch God move. He didn't disappoint. Healings, signs, wonders, and miracles were commonplace in Woodworth-Etter's meetings.

Of course, miracles always draw crowds and critics, and it was no different for this female pioneer. However, she didn't see the attacks from fellow healing evangelist John Alexander Dowie coming. Dowie, himself moving in miracles, at first praised Woodworth-Etter but soon accused her of propagating a great delusion because people were falling into trances left and right under her tent. He called it "trance evangelism."

Woodworth-Etter also drew attention from the media. The *Salem* report documents her falling into a trance on March 24, 1904, and she "had to be laid on the platform for over an hour." The *Indianapolis Star* also reported "Woodworth-Etter Goes into a Trance" in a 1904 edition. In 1913, The *Boston Globe* reported, "Took No Money for Healing; Mrs. Etter Gave God Credit for Cures."[6]

There are accounts of Woodworth-Etter falling into a trance at a St. Louis meeting and standing like a statue for three whole days as attendees of the World Fair looked on in amazement. It's not clear if the trance actually lasted that long, but she was known to fall into trances that left her frozen for hours at a time—and so did many others who attended her meetings.

"People fell into trances, experienced visions of heaven and hell, collapsed on the floor as if they'd been shot or had died," reports Revival Library. "Thousands were healed of a wide variety of sicknesses and diseases and many believers, even ministers, received mighty baptisms of the Holy Spirit."

Often, unbelievers who came in to disrupt the service were encountered by the power of God and themselves fell into a trance. Reporters ridiculed her, her husband lashed out at her in a public letter, she lost the support of well-known ministers in her day, but she continued preaching the Gospel and people continued getting saved—and falling into trances. Woodworth-Etter pointed people to scriptural references of trances and believed it was the power of God.

Criticized in her day, she goes down in Pentecostal history as a pioneer, a forerunner who withstood strong persecution to steward the glory of God in her meetings. We need more like Woodworth-Etter in this hour.

In the *Weekly Evangel*, Robert J. Craig, an early Pentecostal leader and pastor of Glad Tidings Temple in San Francisco, honored her and encouraged ministers to study her life and ministry: "If the Pentecostal ministry would study her life and count on God, expecting the supernatural to be revealed in each meeting, what a mighty agency ours would be in the hands of God."

Amen. And think about it for a minute. What would happen if skeptics of the gospel entered a Holy Ghost meeting and fell into a trance and saw visions of hell? Maybe trance evangelism isn't such a bad idea.

How to Enter the Trance Realm

You can't choose to enter an ecstatic realm trance any more than you can choose to have a God-inspired dream. Look at the biblical examples. Balaam didn't ask God to bring him into a trance. Peter did not ask God to bring him into a trance. Paul did not ask God to bring him into a trance. It was a God-ordained suddenly that they couldn't have expected and one that left a mark on them. Usually, people who fall into God-given trances are emotional or have strong memories about the experience.

Given biblical precedent and the reality of demonic agents who seek to enter trances for wicked purposes, I don't believe we should ask the Lord to put us into trances. God does tell us to pursue spiritual gifts, but a trance is not a gift like the nine gifts of the Spirit, which was the context by which the Holy Spirit inspired Paul to inspire us to pursue them. If we seek supernatural experiences for the sake of supernatural experiences, the devil will oblige. At the same time, we do not want to quench the spirit through fear, unbelief, or doubt. Be open to anything God wants to do for you, give to you, or take from you and you'll experience everything He has for you in the right time and the right season.

Pray this prayer with me, "Father, thank You for teaching me about the trance realm. I am open and ready for any realm You want to show me, but I do not want to go where You aren't taking me. Help me not to be deceived by false encounters and demonic realms. Open my eyes only to what You want to show me, in Jesus' name."

Chapter 11

The Out-of-Body Dimension

John the Revelator was caught up in the Lord's day. Out of this ecstatic encounter came the Book of Revelation, with its many overwhelming visions of the end-times, angelic activity, and a picture of the return of the Lord Himself. This ecstatic encounter occurred while John was in exile on the island of Patmos. He describes it this way:

> *I, John, both your brother and companion in the tribulation and kingdom and patience of Jesus Christ, was on the island that is called Patmos for the word of God and for the testimony of Jesus Christ. I was in the Spirit on the Lord's Day, and I heard behind me a loud voice, as of a trumpet, saying, "I am the Alpha and the Omega, the First and the Last," and, "What you see, write in a book and send it to the seven churches which are in Asia: to Ephesus, to Smyrna, to Pergamos, to Thyatira, to Sardis, to Philadelphia, and to Laodicea. Then I turned to see the voice that spoke with me"* (Revelation 1:9–12).

John has four experiences in the Book of Revelation where he says he's in this spirit (see Rev. 1:10; 4:2; 17:3; 21:10). In one of those instances he says an angel carried him away in the Spirit. What does this phrase "in the Spirit" mean? It means that while John was physically in Patmos, his spirt was somewhere else. This is the same experience Paul had and the same experience Ezekiel had several times:

> *Then the Spirit lifted me up, and I heard behind me a loud rumbling sound as the glory of the Lord rose from the place where it was standing. It was the sound of the wings of the living creatures brushing against each other and the sound of the wheels beside them, a loud rumbling sound. The Spirit then lifted me up and took me away, and I went in bitterness and in the anger of my spirit, with the strong hand of the Lord on me (Ezekiel 3:12–14 NIV).*

Another time, Ezekiel records: "*He stretched out the form of a hand, and took me by a lock of my hair; and the Spirit lifted me up between earth and heaven, and brought me in visions of God to Jerusalem, to the door of the north gate of the inner court, where the seat of the image of jealousy was, which provokes to jealousy*" (Ezek. 8:3). And again in Ezekiel 43:5, he writes, "*The Spirit lifted me up and brought me into the inner court; and behold, the glory of the Lord filled the temple.*"

Paul described his own out-of-body experience in 2 Corinthians 12:2–4:

> *I know a man in Christ who fourteen years ago—whether in the body I do not know, or whether out of the body I do not know, God knows—such a one was caught up to the third heaven. And I know such a man—whether in the body or out of the body I do not know, God knows—how he was caught up into Paradise and heard inexpressible words, which it is not lawful for a man to utter.*

When Kenneth Hagin was Caught Up

Today we don't hear as much about people getting caught up in the Spirit. That may be because many who are in the secret place with God don't have public platforms that gain international attention. Kenneth Hagin Sr., founder of the Word of Faith movement, recorded an encounter he had that's worth noting. Here is his account of being "lost in the spirit."

> After the final service of Campmeeting '79 this past July, some of the speakers and others went up to Kenneth Hagin Jr.'s hotel suite for sandwiches.
>
> As we were talking about the things of God, the Spirit of God kept moving on me. (Actually, only three times in my life has the Spirit moved on me in such a measure.)
>
> I said to the others, "Let's pray. The Spirit of God keeps moving on me."
>
> We prayed. By the Spirit, I ministered to each one present. Then I was caught up in the spirit of prayer and intercession. For lack of a better term, I was "lost in the spirit." I was not unconscious—but I was more conscious of spiritual things. Spiritual things were more real than the natural.
>
> I sat with my eyes shut, praying in tongues, for what proved to be several hours. (It was just after midnight when we started praying. When it was all over, and I opened my eyes, it was after 4 a.m. Yet it seemed as if it had been only 10 or 15 minutes.)
>
> The Lord spoke to me. Among other things, He gave me instructions concerning the Prayer and Healing School we are now holding every week day afternoon on the RHEMA Bible Training campus.

And I saw something. I saw three things coming up out of the Atlantic Ocean. They looked like three giant black frogs, as large as whales. One was already in midair. The other two had just stuck their heads up out of the water from the east. I had seen something similar nine years before.

Jesus said to me, "You saw the same thing in 1970. I told you then exactly what they were, but you didn't do what you should have done about it. I told you back in 1970 to pray for the leaders of the nation. What happened [Watergate and so forth] isn't all the fault of the man who was then President. I am going to hold the Christians of this nation responsible. You are the ones who allowed what happened to your nation. If you had prayed, it never would have happened. I showed you what was about to happen. Go back and check...."

(Later, I went back and checked what the Lord had said to me in 1970 from tapes and manuscripts of a special meeting we held in October 1970.)[1]

Traveling in the Spirit

You've watched science fiction movies that focus on time travel. Traveling in the Spirit is not time travel, but it does interrupt the cycle of time because God can transport someone from one place to another at any given moment in time. Traveling in the Spirit is an ecstatic state. One of the clearest examples of Spirit travel in the Bible is found in the Book of Acts.

We see the Holy Spirit whisking Philip away on assignment after he ministered the Gospel to the Ethiopian eunuch passing through Jerusalem. After the eunuch got saved, Philip baptized him in water and was suddenly gone: *"Now when they came up out of the water, the Spirit of the Lord caught Philip away, so that the eunuch saw him no more; and he went on his way rejoicing. But Philip was found at Azotus. And passing through, he preached in all the cities till he came to Caesarea"* (Acts 8:39–40).

Some Bible commentators insist the Holy Spirit merely urged Philip to go to Azotus immediately after this event so he wouldn't be overly invested in the life of the eunuch. But Matthew Poole's commentary reveals, "Philip was suddenly and extraordinarily taken away from the eunuch's sight and company, that thereby the eunuch might be the more assured of the truth of those things which had been taught by him."[2]

And *Gill's Exposition of the Entire Bible* tells us, "The Spirit of the Lord took up Philip, just as he is said to lift up Ezekiel, between earth and heaven, (Ezekiel 8:3) and carried him above the earth as far as Azotus. The Alexandrian copy, and one of Baez's, and some others, read the words thus, 'the holy Spirit fall upon the eunuch, but the angel of the Lord caught away Philip.'"[3]

If Elijah was taken to Heaven—raptured before he died—and he was, then it should not be difficult to believe the same Holy Spirit could take Peter instantly to another city. And it should not be difficult to believe the Holy Spirit can do the same today, since God does not change.

Patricia King has traveled in the Spirit. She gives an account on Sid Roth's *It's Supernatural!* months before she went to Jerusalem for the first time in the natural, she explains, she was in prayer for Israel. As she was praying the Spirit, God took her into what she calls a visionary encounter or a transvision. She ended up in the city of Jerusalem, then found herself flying through the streets of Jerusalem interceding for the peace of Jerusalem.

"It was so real and tangible that I actually smelled like fragrances, like spices and that, and I could actually feel wind against my face. I acknowledged the wind of the city, the warm wind of the city blowing against my face," King says. "And it was months later when I actually went to Israel for my first time, and I was walking through the streets of Jerusalem that I realized this is where I was in the spirit, the same smells, the fragrance, the feel of the air. And it was just a very surreal time. It was awesome."

King also describes another ecstatic encounter that occurred when she was in Mesa, Arizona. Her friend was in the hospital in Vancouver, British Columbia, fifteen hundred miles away. She got a call from her friend's daughter saying, "Please pray for my mother. She is very sick." The diagnoses didn't sound good: pulmonary embolism. As King was walking down the street praying for her friend, she was transported in the Spirit to the hospital where her friend was.

"I actually saw her in the hospital bed.... And the Holy Spirit had told me to release by faith the healing blessing. And so I just by faith released that blessing. It was just an act of faith. And then immediately I was back on the street of Mesa, Arizona, where I had been walking. I thought, 'Oh my gosh, I was just in Vancouver over my friend's body in the hospital imparting healing.' I knew that I knew that I knew that she was healed," says King. And her friend was healed.[4]

The purpose of traveling in the Spirit is not for a great story, but a great move of God. People can be saved, healed, and delivered through ecstatic encounters of this kind.

Entering Deep Sleep

Entering into a deep sleep is an ecstatic encounter that few speak of. This is not the dream realm, rather, a deeper state than normal sleep where you do not remember the experience. We see God put Adam in a deep sleep when he pulled out a rib to form a woman. We also see Abraham and Daniel enter this kind of encounter. Look at what happened to Abraham:

Now when the sun was going down, a deep sleep fell upon Abram; and behold, horror and great darkness fell upon him. Then He said to Abram: "Know certainly that your descendants will be strangers in a land that is not theirs, and will serve them, and they will afflict them four hundred years. And also the nation whom they serve I will judge; afterward they shall come out with great possessions. Now as for you, you shall go to your fathers in peace; you shall be buried at a good old age. But in the fourth generation they shall return here, for the iniquity of the Amorites is not yet complete." And it came to pass, when the sun went down and it was dark, that behold, there appeared a smoking oven and a burning torch that passed between those pieces (Genesis 15:12–17).

THE SECRET DIMENSION

E veryone—even God—has secrets. Choosing whether to reveal a secret—and to whom—rests solely in the power of the secret holder. In the secret dimension, God is the revealer of secrets (see Dan. 2:47). We know God reveals His secrets to two different types of people—His servants the prophets and those who fear Him (see Amos 3:7; Ps. 25:14).

You have the inherent potential to enter the secret dimension of the seer realm as a born-again believer. Deuteronomy 29:29 tells us, *"The secret things belong to the Lord our God, but those things which are revealed belong to us and to our children forever, that we may do all the words of this law."*

The unfortunate reality is few will enter into the secret dimension because they are unaware of its existence or they won't pay the price to cultivate a lifestyle that gains them access. God can share His secrets with us through a still small voice or through the seer dimension—encounters, trances, dreams, and visions.

We find many types of secrets spoken of in the pages of the Bible—and there are many more we can discover through our pursuit of the

Holy One of Israel. Understanding what's scripturally available to you builds faith to access the secret dimension of the seer world.

Seeing Secret Places in the Spirit World

Most Christians have felt the presence of God, and because God is omnipresent technically we are always in His presence. But there is a deeper seer dimension called the secret of God's presence. In Psalm 31:20, David shares: *"You shall hide them in the secret place of Your presence from the plots of man; You shall keep them secretly in a pavilion from the strife of tongues."*

Many scriptures point us to this secret place. Psalm 91:1 assures us, *"He who dwells in the secret place of the Most High shall abide under the shadow of the Almighty."* When you enter the secret place of God's presence in the seer realm, you will see strong angelic activity. You will no longer hear the strife of tongues, you will hear the song of the Lord, the sounds of angels, or one of the many diverse and otherworldly sights and sounds. Several times I have entered into this secret dimension and heard angels singing or spiritual frequencies I cannot describe. I often hear high-pitched frequencies in the spirit that alert me to significant angelic activity.

The secret place of thunder is a phenomenon few seem to experience—and it's fascinating. In Psalm 81:7 the Lord says to David, *"You called in trouble, and I delivered you; I answered you in the secret place of thunder."* The word for "thunder" in that verse literally means thunder. Think about it for a minute. A secret place that is so loud that there's a reverberating rumble? Given thunder always follows lightning, consider the awesome sights of the secret place of thunder.

Thunder is often a sign of judgment. God sent thunder and hailstones against the Egypt when Pharaoh would not let the Israelites go to worship Him (see Exod. 9:23). God thunders against His adversaries (see 1 Sam. 2:10). The Lord thundered with a loud thunder against the Philistines (see 1 Sam. 7:10). The secret place of thunder is a place of protection for the innocent and judgment upon the enemy. When you see lightning in the spirit, it often means thunder is coming against the enemy's camp as God sends lightning bolts to vanquish His enemies (see 2 Sam. 22:15). Ask the Lord to show you, like He showed Elisha's servant, the war in the heavens. Press in to see.

There are also secret places in the demonic dimension about which one should be aware. Psalm 10:8 warns of the innocent murdered in secret places, and Psalm 17:12 speaks of young lions lurking in secret places. As a seer or seeing person, you can see into the secret dimension of demonic activity. This goes beyond simple discernment into a deeper realm that is hidden so deep that most never sense it until it begins to manifest. Ask the Lord to show you enemies hidden in secret places and wait to see.

Noteworthy are the Lord's own words in Jeremiah 23:24: *"Can anyone hide himself in secret places, so I shall not see him?"* If the Lord can see people—even people who are hiding from the light—then He can allow us to see them.

Scripture also warns us of illegal entry into the secret place. In Ezekiel 7:22 God reveals the wicked *"will defile My secret place; for robbers shall enter in and defile it."* Remember, demons come to steal, kill, and destroy (see John 10:10). The enemy wants to rob your purity by tempting you to enter secret places illegally. I teach more about this in the final chapter of this book.

Seeing Hidden Treasures in Secret Places

Treasures and riches are hidden in the spirit realm and seers can access them in the secret dimension as the Lord opens their eyes. Several scriptures point us to these realties and should give us enough spiritual curiosity to ask the Lord to show us for His glory.

In Isaiah 45:3, God gives us a hint about what's available in the secret dimension: *"I will give you the treasures of darkness and hidden riches of secret places."* One of those hidden treasures is likened to wisdom in Proverbs 2:4, which is noteworthy because Job wished God would show his critical friends *"the secrets of wisdom"* (Job 11:6).

Although God will pour out wisdom on those who ask, there are secrets of wisdom that unlock greater wisdom. These often come in the form of keys in the seer realm. When you see keys, look carefully to see if they are marked *wisdom*. Often keys marked *wisdom* have a large oval handle at the top with a thinner shaft.

In The Parable of the Hidden Treasure, Jesus shares a truth that you can meditate on to enter into this seer dimension: *"Again, the kingdom of heaven is like treasure hidden in a field, which a man found and hid; and for joy over it he goes and sells all that he has and buys that field"* (Matt. 13:44).

If you are going to go on a treasure hunt in the secret dimension, start with the Word of God. Remember, He is the revealer of secrets. This dimension should not be avoided. After all, He has given us the power to create wealth to establish His covenant in the earth (see Deut. 8:18) and Proverbs 8:12 speaks of witty inventions. If we can see the hidden treasures and riches, we can be agents of a supernatural wealth transfer to build the kingdom.

Seeing Secret Counsels of God, Man, and the Devil

The Bible speaks of the secret counsel of God and the secret counsel of the wicked. It's strategic to tap into both of these frequencies so you know what God wants to do and what the enemy is plotting and planning.

Proverbs 3:32 tells us God's secret counsel is with the upright. When David reveals the Lord counsels him and instructs his mind at night (see Ps. 16:7) he is tapping into the secret counsel of God. God spoke to David's spirit and his spirit communicates with his mind.

Remember, one of the names of God is Wonderful Counselor (see Isa. 9:6). His secret counsel is wonderful and His counsel stands forever (see Ps. 33:11). The counsel of the Lord always stands (see Prov. 19:21). God often gives us counsel in secret so the enemy is not aware of the wisdom He is imparting to overthrow his wicked plots.

Psalm 64:2 records David crying out to the God of secrets to preserve him from the secret counsel of the wicked. The enemy also has secret counsel—and Elisha demonstrates how the seer gift, by the will of God, can look into the enemy's plans in 2 Kings 6:8-12:

> *Now the king of Syria was making war against Israel; and he consulted with his servants, saying, "My camp will be in such and such a place." And the man of God sent to the king of Israel, saying, "Beware that you do not pass this place, for the Syrians are coming down there." Then the king of Israel sent someone to the place of which the man of God had told him. Thus he warned him, and he was watchful there, not just once or twice. Therefore the heart of the king of Syria was greatly troubled by this thing; and he called his servants and said to them, "Will you not show me which of us is for the king of Israel?" And one of his servants said, "None, my lord, O king; but Elisha, the prophet who is in Israel, tells the king of Israel the words that you speak in your bedroom."*

Someone's bedroom is a private place—a secret place. When people are cursing me or plotting against me, I can often see in the spirit who it is and hear what they are saying. This seer insight gives me the opportunity to break the back of the enemy's plot, bless those who curse me, and pray for those who are coming against me. When we enter into the secret realm, we can expose the secret plots of the enemy. We can uproot, tear down, destroy, and overthrow the enemy's plots so we can build and plant God's will in our lives, churches, cities, and nations.

Seeing Secrets of the Heart

At times, we can see the secrets of men—the secrets of their heart and even secret sins. Psalm 44:21 tells us God knows the secrets of the heart. Of course, God knows everything from our unspoken prayers to our unpursued desires and beyond. He sees the secrets of sinners and saints alike. Nothing is hidden from Him. In the realm of prophecy, we must tread in this secret dimension with caution. We can be helpful or harmful.

Paul explains how to deal with sinners in seeing the secrets of the heart in 1 Corinthians 14:24-25: *"But if all prophesy, and an unbeliever or an uninformed person comes in, he is convinced by all, he is convicted by all. And thus the secrets of his heart are revealed; and so, falling down on his face, he will worship God and report that God is truly among you."* Seeing the secrets of a sinner's heart and prophesying God's love and will can bring about salvation.

In this seer dimension, you may see the good or the bad. Never call out the dirt, but always focus on the treasure. The enemy can easily fool you into projecting your own sin onto another's life. When the Pharisees dragged forth a woman caught in the act of adultery, Jesus was clear: He who has no sin should cast the first stone (see John 8:7).

I met a woman at my school of prophets and seers in Los Angeles who said she saw people's sins written across their foreheads and it overwhelmed her. My advice: pray for them using the knowledge you gained by seeing the secret sin. Psalm 90:8 speaks of secret sins and Romans 2:16 speaks of a day when God will judge the secrets of men. But it is not our place as seers and seeing people to judge. If you see secret sins, make intercession. Don't judge because it will cause a beam to be formed in your eye and hinder your ability to see. You are not sinless. Remember the words of Christ on the Sermon on the Mount in Matthew 7:1-5:

Judge not, that you be not judged. For with what judgment you judge, you will be judged; and with the measure you use, it will be measured back to you. And why do you look at the speck in your brother's eye, but do not consider the plank in your own eye? Or how can you say to your brother, "Let me remove the speck from your eye"; and look, a plank is in your own eye? Hypocrite! First remove the plank from your own eye, and then you will see clearly to remove the speck from your brother's eye.

Entering the Secret Dimension

Entering the secret dimension is not reserved for a few, but fewer enter into it because it demands strong character and trustworthiness. We can't manipulate or force our way into the secret dimension, at least not legally. We can take hints as to what authorizes us to enter in by what the Bible itself says about it. Beyond the obvious suggestion of prayer, here are six keys to entering the secret dimension.

1. Cultivate a Fear of the Lord

One definition of the Hebrew word *yare* means "to fear, to respect, to reverence." The Greek word *phobos* can be translated "reverential fear." *Vine's Complete Expository Dictionary* defines it as "not a mere 'fear' of His power and righteous retribution, but a wholesome dread of displeasing Him." That's intense!

The fear of the Lord is to hate evil (Prov. 8:13). The fear of the Lord is the beginning of wisdom (Prov. 9:10). The fear of the Lord is the beginning of knowledge (Prov. 1:7). The secret of the Lord is with those who fear Him (Ps. 25:14). There is no want for them who fear Him (Ps. 34:9). In the fear of the Lord, there is strong confidence and a fountain of life (Prov. 14:26-27). By the fear of the Lord are riches, honor, and life (Prov. 22:4).

2. Set a Guard Over Your Mouth

Can you keep a secret? Do you have tight lips? Or are you a gossip? Think about it for a minute. Who do you tell your secrets to? If you are like me, you don't share your secrets with blabbermouths. We have to cooperate with the Holy Spirit in taming our tongues. Let this be your prayer: "Set a guard, O Lord, over my mouth; keep watch over the door of my lips."

3. Prove Yourself Trustworthy

Can the Lord trust you? He knows. I share my secrets with people I know I can trust. Keeping my secrets hidden is only one part of the equation. People need to trust you.

4. Determine to See as a Servant

In Amos 3:7, the word *servant* is rarely emphasized. People say, "God shares His secrets with the prophets." But the Scripture says He shares them with *"His servants the prophets."* You can be called a prophet and serve your own agenda with information.

The Hebrew word for "servant" in Amos 3:7 is *ebed.* That word means a servant, worshiper, subject, manservant, and slave, according to *The KJV Old Testament Hebrew Lexicon.* When you see through the eyes of a servant—doing everything as unto the Lord as an act of worship—you will see through the correct lens.

5. Purify Your Motives

Remember, when God opens up the secret dimension to you, it's in order to help you or someone else walk in God's will. If your motive is not pure toward the Lord or toward people—if you plan to use that information to benefit yourself instead of helping people and advancing God's kingdom, you can't enter the secret realm legally.

6. Pursue Intimacy with the Holy Spirit

Keep in mind the word *secret* in Amos 3:7 and Psalm 25:14 comes from the Hebrew word *cowd.* It denotes counsel in "familiar conversation" and speaks of "familiar friends," according to *The KJV Old Testament Hebrew Lexicon.* When you're building relationships with people, you have to make yourself available—even when it's not convenient to you. Sometimes intimacy means sacrifice. Many people want to walk in the secret dimension but they don't want to spend time with the revealer of secrets.

CHAPTER 13

THE SILENT DIMENSION

When I was a child I broke my leg and landed in the hospital in a painful traction for weeks. After traction, I was in a full body cast. Just months after I was healed and liberated from the cast, I broke my leg a second time, was once again bound to a hospital bed for months and confined to a body cast for months more.

During these extended periods of immobility, I sat in silence hour after hour, day after day, week after week, and month after month. While my parents were at work, nurses or other caregivers would check in with me only a couple of times a day. To some, that may sound more painful than broken bones and at first it was. But I learned to enjoy silence. I discovered the benefits of silence. I relished the power of silence. In recent years, I've discovered how silence fuels the seer gift.

Silence is the absence of sound, but it's also a dimension in the spirit where one receives revelation from the throne room. Learning how to remain quiet in soul and calm in spirit in order to discern what is happening in the spirit world and see what the Lord is saying is vital to navigating seer dimensions.

St. John of the Cross, a major figure in the Spanish Counter-Reformation, is known as a friend of silence. He wrote things like: "Carve out a day every week, or an hour a day, or a moment each hour, and abide in loving silence with the Friend. Feel the frenetic concerns of life in the world fall away, like the last leaves of autumn being lifted from the tree in the arms of a zephyr. Be the bare tree."[1]

"It is best to learn to silence the faculties and to cause them to be still so that God may speak," he wrote.[2] "What we need most in order to make progress is to be silent before this great God with our appetite and with our tongue, for the language he best hears is silent love."[3]

It's been said by many mystics and seers that silence is God's first language. Silence can be uncomfortable at times but it is a powerful pursuit that brings clarity of vision. Psalm 46:10: *"Be still, and know that I am God."* This heart posture will position you to enter the silent realm.

Contemplating in Silence

Silence is the foundation of contemplative prayer. Contemplative prayer opens your eyes in ways other prayer does not because it leads you into intimacy with God, the source of all revelation. Some in modern times call this soaking prayer. I prefer contemplative. Contemplative prayer is about intimacy with God, who is the Ultimate Seer. Contemplative prayer is centuries old and is actually rooted in monks, hermits, and nuns. I do not agree with the doctrines of the Catholic church, but the reality is those who set themselves apart in His presence lived from the inside out.

"The Protestant wing of the western church, which is a tiny percentage of the Body of Christ, is nearly completely (98%) unaware that the Holy Spirit is restoring contemplative prayer—center stage—to the church. The Holy Spirit is restoring this precious jewel (contemplative prayer) to the body of Christ," says Mike Bickle, founder of IHOPKC.[4] "This is the God ordained means of attaining the fullness of God."

There is some controversy around this, but not by intimate lovers of Jesus. Even Focus on the Family, a conservative evangelical Christian organization, agrees with the realities of contemplative prayer, writing: "There is nothing unbiblical or anti-Christian about solitude, silence, and contemplative prayer. Not, at any rate, as they have been practiced *within the context of Christian history.* As a matter of fact, these disciplines are part of a time-honored tradition. They've been central to the church's spiritual life for centuries."⁵

Defining Contemplative Prayer

If you ask ten leaders what contemplative prayer is, you may get ten different answers. There's no one standard definition. Let's start by understanding the word *contemplative*, which is related to contemplation. Contemplation is "a concentration on spiritual things as a form of private devotion or a state of mystical awareness of God's being," according to *Merriam-Webster's Dictionary.* It's an act of considering with attention, regarding steadily with intention and expectation.

Contemplative prayer is an ancient Christian practice that dates all the way back to the early church and even to the life of King David. The psalms give proof of David's contemplative prayer life. David wrote, *"I will meditate on Your precepts, and contemplate Your ways"* (Ps. 119:15).

Contemplative prayer is a thoughtful practice where you focus on the Word of God to the point where you drown out other thoughts, feelings, and temporal distractions. You are focusing on the Father, Son, and Holy Spirit *within* you rather than the Father, Son, and Holy Spirit outside of you. God's voice becomes clearer through this practice.

Mike Bickle defines contemplative prayer as "prayer that focuses on enjoying intimacy with God." In contemplative prayer, we behold God's glory and we are transformed into His image (see 2 Cor. 3:18). In Psalm 27:4, David said he just wanted one thing—to behold God's beauty. Beholding God's beauty is the same as beholding His glory. Contemplative prayer releases the Holy Spirit's supernatural activity in our spirits as we encounter His heart. We enter into enjoyable communion with God that transforms us.

James Goll, founder of God Encounters Ministries and author of *The Seer*, wrote in an article, "Contemplative prayer has too often been relegated to ancient church history. But God is restoring it as a means to develop intimacy with Him. I have found that the most direct road to greater intimacy with God has come through the practice or discipline of an almost-lost art in the fast-paced church of today—something called contemplative prayer."[6]

Saint John of the Cross, a 16th century monk, said, "For contemplation is nothing else than a secret and peaceful and loving inflow of God, which, if not hampered, fires the soul in the spirit of love."[7] And Teresa of Avila wrote, "Contemplative prayer [oración mental] in my opinion is nothing else than a close sharing between friends; it means taking time frequently to be alone with him who we know loves us."[8]

Ray Simpson puts it this way: "Contemplative prayer is natural, unprogrammed; it is perpetual openness to God, so that in the openness his concerns can flow in and out of our minds as he wills."[9] David Bentley Hart explains: "As an old monk on Mount Athos once told me, contemplative prayer is the art of seeing reality as it truly is; and, if one has not yet acquired the ability to see God in all things, one should not imagine that one will be able to see God in himself."[10]

Silent Seeking is Intimacy

The silent dimension and contemplative prayer are about seeking God and His kingdom. Matthew 6:33 promises rewards to those who practice this discipline of seeking. Jesus said:

> *Therefore do not worry and be anxious, saying, What are we going to have to eat? or, What are we going to have to drink? or, What are we going to have to wear? For the Gentiles*

(heathen) wish for and crave and diligently seek all these things, and your heavenly Father knows well that you need them all. But seek (aim at and strive after) first of all His kingdom and His righteousness (His way of doing and being right), and then all these things taken together will be given you besides (Matthew 6:31-33 AMPC).

Jesus is speaking of natural provision in these verses, but the same holds true for spiritual food, spiritual drink, and spiritual mantles. We know God as a rewarder of those who diligently seek Him (see Heb. 11:6). In Psalm 27:8, David said, *"When You said, 'Seek My face,' my heart said to You, 'Your face, Lord, I will seek.'"* Even as I pen these words, I am hearing the Lord say, "Seek Me and you will find Me; you will find treasures of darkness in secret places; you will find the keys to mysteries in My kingdom. You will see these things because the Holy Spirit will show them forth to those who are diligent and upright in heart."

It's all about intimacy. Cultivating the oil of intimacy in our lives requires time in God's presence, as well as renewing our minds with scriptures about who we are in Christ and His love for us. We must have faith and confidence in our position in Him. We gain intimacy with God by studying His emotions; through praising, worshiping and fellowshipping with Him; and by determining to seek, obey, and please Him in our thoughts, words, and deeds. When we seek to abide in Him, we are cultivating the oil of intimacy.

Reading the Song of Solomon reveals the love God has for us in a beautiful allegory. In our pursuit of intimacy, we need to gain a revelation of Jesus as not only King and Judge, but also Bridegroom. Consider these scriptures that reveal God's emotions for us, understanding that a revelation of His heart for us is what fuels our desire for more of Him.

You shall no more be termed Forsaken, nor shall your land be termed Desolate; but you shall be called My Delight Is In

Her, and your land Married; for the Lord delights in you, and your land shall be married. For as a young man marries a virgin, so your sons shall marry you; and as the bridegroom rejoices over the bride, so your God shall rejoice over you (Isaiah 62:4-5 MEV).

You have ravished my heart, my sister, my bride; you have ravished my heart with one glance of your eyes, with one jewel of your necklace. How fair is your love, my sister, my bride! How much better than wine is your love, and the fragrance of your oils than any spice! (Song of Songs 4:9-10 MEV)

My beloved is mine, and I am his (Song of Songs 2:16).

As the Father loved Me, I also loved you. Remain in My love (John 15:9 MEV).

Indeed, I have loved you with an everlasting love; therefore with lovingkindness I have drawn you (Jeremiah 31:3 MEV).

I have given them the glory which You gave Me, that they may be one even as We are one: I in them and You in Me, that they may be perfect in unity, and that the world may know that You have sent Me, and have loved them as You have loved Me (John 17:22-23 MEV).

The Lord your God is in your midst, a Mighty One, who will save. He will rejoice over you with gladness, He will renew you with His love, He will rejoice over you with singing (Zephaniah 3:17 MEV).

We need to become people of one thing, like David, who said:

One thing have I asked of the Lord, that will I seek, inquire for, and [insistently] require: that I may dwell in the house of the Lord [in His presence] all the days of my life, to behold and gaze upon the beauty [the sweet attractiveness and the delightful loveliness] of the Lord and to meditate, consider, and inquire in His temple (Psalm 27:4 AMPC).

Intimacy demands silence, meditation, and contemplation over busyness. There is a time for every purpose under heaven. There's a time to work and a time rest. There's a time to speak and a time to remain silent (see Eccles. 3:7). Read the account in Luke 10:38-42 and consider your own lifestyle:

> *Now it happened as they went that He entered a certain village; and a certain woman named Martha welcomed Him into her house. And she had a sister called Mary, who also sat at Jesus' feet and heard His word. But Martha was distracted with much serving, and she approached Him and said, "Lord, do You not care that my sister has left me to serve alone? Therefore tell her to help me." And Jesus answered and said to her, "Martha, Martha, you are worried and troubled about many things. But one thing is needed, and Mary has chosen that good part, which will not be taken away from her."*

Martha didn't discern the times correctly and wound up frustrated while Mary enjoyed intimacy with Jesus. Martha was noisy in her complaints. Mary was silent before Jesus.

J. Brent Bill, author of *Holy Silence: The Gift of Quaker Spirituality*, drives home this point:

> When we really want to hear, and be heard by, someone we love, we do not go rushing into noisy crowds. Silence is a form of intimacy. That's how we experience it with our friends and lovers. As relationships grow deeper and more

intimate, we spend more and more quiet time alone with our lover. We talk in low tones about the things that matter. We do not shout them to each other. We may shout about them to others, but quietness is the hallmark of love.[11]

Entering the Silent Dimension

You can enter the silent dimension, the silence of God, through contemplative prayer. James Goll explains:

> Contemplative prayer immerses us into the silence of God and helps us let go of control of our own life that leans on the props of this world for fulfillment. It is communion with God that increases our awareness of His presence. As we become more aware of His presence we are more willing to submit to the Holy Spirit's cleansing work of purification bringing us to a place of surrender.[12]

Find a Quiet Place

It's not impossible to enter the silent dimension in a noisy place, but it's much easier to seclude yourself away from the distractions of life. It can be frustrating to enter the silent dimension and have something or someone pull you out of an encounter or vision. Jesus went to a quiet place early in the morning to seek the Father and pray in silence (see Mark 1:35).

Close Your Eyes

You don't have to close your eyes to enter the silent dimension or practice contemplative prayer, but, again, this can help you focus without distraction.

Calm and Quiet Your Soul

You can sit in quiet and close your eyes and still have mind traffic racing through your soul. David said, *"Surely I have calmed and quieted my soul"* (Ps. 131:2). That word "quieted" in the Hebrew is *daman*. It means "to be silent, be still, wait, be dumb, grow dumb," according to *The KJV Old Testament Hebrew Lexicon*.

For many people, this is the hardest part of entering the silent dimension. You can quiet your soul by taking deep breaths. Slowing your breathing calms the whole body. Playing instrumental worship music can help quiet your mind as it distracts your mind from thoughts without ultimately distracting you from God. Reciting a scripture in your mind over and over again, as well as gazing on the Lord's beauty, can also help quiet your mind.

Receive in Silence

Once you have quieted your mind, you are positioned to meditate and contemplate at a deeper level. This is when you can expect to start seeing and hearing with greater clarity.

As Andrew Murray wrote, "Here is the secret of a life of prayer. Take time in the inner chamber to bow down and worship; and wait on Him until He unveils Himself, and takes possession of you, and goes out with you to show how a man can live and walk in abiding fellowship with an unseen Lord."[13]

Chapter 14

Meditation: A Master Key to Mystical Dimensions

I was meditating on Revelation 4:1 again and again. I read it over and over. I pondered each word. I spoke it out loud. Revelation 4:1 reads, *"After these things I looked, and behold, a door standing open in heaven. And the first voice which I heard was like a trumpet speaking with me, saying, 'Come up here, and I will show you things which must take places after this.'"*

I don't know how long I was meditating on that verse. I lost track of time as I focused in with deeper meditation on a few specific words and phrases in that verse. The words *looked, behold, door standing open,* and *come up here* seemed to leap off the page and into my heart, somehow bypassing my natural mind. It was as if the spirit of the word was entering my spirit by osmosis.

My thoughts were, "If there is an open door in heaven, I want to walk through it." Suddenly, I saw myself walking toward a magnificent castle. I saw a large opening with a walkway that ran directly through the castle. As I walked to the midway point of what seemed to be a sacred path, the castle rolled up and went inside my spirit.

In that moment I heard the Lord say, "The kingdom of God is within you. Everything you need is within you. All the resources you require are within you. You don't even have to pull it down from heaven. It is within you. Speak it out of your mouth and you will see it. Christ in you, the hope of glory. The riches in glory in Christ are within you."

As I had never experienced anything like this before, I found it strange and was not sure what to think about it. I knew it was a spiritual encounter. I knew it was the voice of the Lord. When I began to study this experience, I found Teresa of Avila, a Spanish woman who chose a monastic lifestyle in the 16th century. She was set apart for the Lord and wrote a book called *The Interior Castle.*

Through my experience and her writing, I discovered the way into this castle is prayer and medication. Teresa of Avila wrote:

> As far as I can understand, the door of entry into this castle is prayer and meditation: I do not say mental prayer rather than vocal, for, if it is prayer at all, it must be accompanied by meditation. If a person does not think Whom he is addressing, and what he is asking for, and who it is that is asking and of Whom he is asking it, I do not consider that he is praying at all even though he be constantly moving his lips. True, it is sometimes possible to pray without paying heed to these things, but that is only because they have been thought about previously; if a man is in the habit of speaking to God's Majesty as he would speak to his slave, and never wonders if he is expressing himself properly, but merely utters the words that come to his lips because he has learned them by heart through constant repetition, I do not call that prayer at all—and God grant no Christian may ever speak to Him so![1]

New Age Did Not Invent Meditation

Many Christians hear the word *meditate* and immediately relegate it to the realm of New Age or Buddhism. But God invented the concept. Meditation is "the act of calling to mind some supposition, pondering upon it, and correlating it to one's own life," according to *Holman Bible Dictionary*, and is at its root an act of worship.

We can release meditation in many forms. The Hebrew word for "meditate" is *hagah*. It means to utter, muse, mutter, meditate, speak, or imagine," according to *The KJV Old Testament Hebrew Lexicon*.[2] You meditate by thinking about the same image or speaking the same words repeatedly.

The first mention of meditation in the Bible is in the Book of Beginnings—Genesis 24:63, *"Isaac went out to meditate in the field in the evening."* In a transition between the loss of his mother and the reception of his bride, *Matthew Henry's Commentary* says, "He went out to take the advantage of a silent evening, and a solitary place, for meditation and prayer; those divine exercises by which we converse with God and our own hearts."

You can meditate anytime, anywhere, but solitude is the best place to move into this dimension of worship. David said, *"I call to remembrance my song in the night; I meditate within my heart, and my spirit makes diligent search"* (Ps. 77:6). When you meditate on the things of God, your spirit is searching the deep things of God while your mind is simultaneously being renewed.

Some people have a hard time practicing the concept of meditation. Don't overcomplicate it. If you know how to ruminate, you know how to meditate. When we have a problem or worry, we ruminate on it. That is to say, to rehash it or review it repeatedly in our thoughts and words. The enemy wants us to meditate on him and his work to kill, steal, and destroy in our lives. God wants us to meditate on Him and His work to bring us into abundance and overflow of His promises.

Delight Yourself in the Word

Because Jesus is the only legitimate door into the seer dimensions, meditating on the Word is the best—and safest—place to start with meditation. Throughout the psalms of David, we see his dedication to meditation. He starts off in Psalm 1:2 talking about the godly man: *"His delight is in the law of the Lord, and in His law he meditates day and night"* (Ps. 1:2). When you set your heart to meditate on His Word day and night you will find easier entry into seer dimensions.

We won't meditate on His Word unless we delight ourselves in the Word. As I write this, I am delighting myself in the Word. When I read the Word, or in this case write about the Word, I am filled with joy because I can see the inherent power in it to change me, to empower me, to comfort me—and to take me places in the seer dimension I could not go alone without risk of error. There is no error in the Word of God, so Word meditation is one gateway through which we can safely enter seer dimensions.

Discipline yourself to do what David did:—meditate on His precepts and have respect for His ways (see Ps. 119:15). Delight in the law of the Lord (see Ps. 1:2). His testimonies should be our delight and our counselor (see Ps. 119:24). Let us never forget that the one who fears the Lord and delights greatly in His commandments is blessed (see Ps. 112:1).

As you can see, delighting in the Word of God is a continual theme throughout the Book of Psalms. But what does it mean to delight yourself in the Word? Do you really know? Delighting is not complicated, but it's important to understand just what the Word of God is telling us to do so that we can do it indeed. Simply stated, to delight in something is to take great pleasure in it. When you are delighted, you are highly pleased. You have joy and satisfaction. The Word of God should be a source of joy. It should satisfy the soul. It should delight you—and it will if you truly know the Word.

Anyone can read the Word and receive information. Receiving revelation in the spirit realm and seer dimensions depends, in part, on our active pursuit of the *logos* (written Word) until it becomes *rhema* (spoken word) to us. As we meditate on the Word, thinking about it, speaking it, and being doers of it, we gain spiritual understanding of seer realities and legalities.

Gaze on His Beauty

Beyond meditating on His Word, we need to meditate on who the Father is, who Christ is, and who the Holy Spirit is. We need to renew our minds to the character and personality of the three Persons of the Trinity. We need to cultivate intimacy with them. Barbie Breathitt, author of *Gateway to the Seer Realm*, writes:

> Seers are called to relate to God through the intimacy of faith, hope, and love. An atmosphere of peaceful meditation allows seers to enter into the spiritual perception of visionary sight. They are able to gaze into the invisible realms of glory and behold the beauty of the Lord, and so are you! David said it this way: One thing I have asked from the Lord, that I shall seek: That I may dwell in the house of the Lord all the days of my life, to behold the beauty of the Lord and to meditate in His temple (Psalm 27:4).
>
> Beholding Jesus or "meditating upon His Word" is the act that brings transformation to the heart and mind. For what we behold, we become (see Joshua 1:8, Romans 12:2, and 2 Corinthians 3:18). So let us gaze at the beautiful Son!
>
> Ra'ah means "to look and see as in a vision, to gaze, view, experience, look upon, behold, discern, or to perceive by the Spirit." Chozeh means "to behold a vision, stargazer,

or to gaze into the realm of the Spirit with approval and agreement, a prophet that sees, a seer."

Seers receive revelation beforehand as they wait upon the Lord's powerful, manifested presence. Their revelations come through their ability to rest in the realm of visions, dreams, pictures, lights, angelic messengers, and trances.

I regularly experience this type of revelatory phenomenon. For me, it takes quiet times of worship, extended peace and solitude, meditation on His Word, and a hushed reflection on the presence of the Lord. Once I am able to still my mind my spirit begins to release love toward God. When I feel His love moving on me, I begin to soak in an atmosphere of panoramic visions. The revelations I have received for my books, messages, and articles come through these quality alone times while resting in the Holy Spirit's presence.[3]

I was once riddled with a spirit of fear. My entire life was filtered through these lenses—even what I saw and heard in the spirit realm. Where others saw angels, I saw dark demons. Where others heard words of encouragement, I heard nothing but warnings of demonic attacks. Although what I was seeing and hearing was accurate, I had a bent toward fear so I could not see beyond the dark side of the spirit.

Once I renewed my mind with the Word of God and received deliverance, my prophetic revelations found balance. Once I moved beyond the warfare-only paradigm and understood the intimacy paradigm, I walked in balance and everything changed.

When I had a dream of a spiritual attack, I saw how the Lord wanted to intervene so I could make intercession accordingly. When I got a revelation of the love of God, which casts out all fear, I was able to see God even in the darkest circumstances, which makes me a more effective prayer warrior. I don't typically see angels in all their glory, but I bumped into one in my kitchen the other day and looked up as a flash of light ascended.

Imagine Scenes in the Bible

Imagination is another aspect of the seer dimension New Agers have hijacked and, in many ways, stolen from the Body of Christ. God created you in His image. God has an imagination and so do you. Imagination is both a creative ability and power to see images in your mind's eye. Imagination is in the realm of the unseen world.

When your spirit was born again, you gained the ability to see all things possible (see Mark 9:23) within the bounds of your imagination. While the enemy tries to use your imagination against you—launching vain imaginations against your mind according to 2 Corinthians 10:5— you can cooperate with God to use your imagination for His glory. As you seek to enter the seer dimensions through the imagination, be careful to first work to root out corrupted areas of your imagination so you can separate what is your own invention from God's innovation.

While reading visions, dreams, parables, and dramatic scenes in the pages of your Bible, meditate on them and use your holy imagination to picture the scenes. If you are diligent about doing this, the Lord could show you exactly what John saw in the Book of Revelation or what Jesus was writing in the sand when the Pharisees sought to condemn the woman who was caught in the act of adultery.

Meditate on Your Legal Position

Take some time to meditate on Ephesians 2:6 in various translations. This will not only renew your mind to your legal position, but inspire you to pursue operating in seer dimensions part of your living condition. Remember, seers and seeing people are in a position to look down to the earth realm from heavenly dimensions.

And God raised us up with Christ and seated us with him in the heavenly realms in Christ Jesus (NIV).

He also raised us up with him and seated us with him in the heavens in Christ Jesus (CSB).

God raised us from death to life with Christ Jesus, and he has given us a place beside Christ in heaven (CEV).

God has brought us back to life together with Christ Jesus and has given us a position in heaven with him (GW).

And He raised us up together with Him and made us sit down together [giving us joint seating with Him] in the heavenly sphere [by virtue of our being] in Christ Jesus (the Messiah, the Anointed One) (AMPC).

He did all this on his own, with no help from us! Then he picked us up and set us down in highest heaven in company with Jesus, our Messiah (MSG).

He raised us up with Christ the exalted One, and we ascended with him into the glorious perfection and authority of the heavenly realm, for we are now co-seated as one with Christ! (TPT)

As you meditate on Ephesians 2:6 and other scriptures, ask the Holy Spirit questions about what you are reading. Ask and keep on asking. Knock and keep on knocking. The Holy Spirit will lead you into all truth (see John 16:13).

Cultivate Spiritual Curiosity

You can meditate on His name; meditate on His wonderful works; meditate on His precepts and ways; and meditate on what is noble, just, pure, lovely, and of a good report (see Mal. 3:16; Ps. 119:15,27; Phil. 4:8). You can, like David did, meditate on God's emotions.

Meditation is only for the spiritually curious. If you aren't hungry, you won't meditate because although it is fascinating to enter seer dimensions through meditation, it requires you to be still and wait on God. It requires a curious spirit set on exploring what God wants to show you.

In Matthew 7:7-11 (AMP), Jesus said:

> *Ask and keep on asking and it will be given to you; seek and keep on seeking and you will find; knock and keep on knocking and the door will be opened to you. For everyone who keeps on asking receives, and he who keeps on seeking finds, and to him who keeps on knocking, it will be opened. Or what man is there among you who, if his son asks for bread, will [instead] give him a stone? Or if he asks for a fish, will [instead] give him a snake? If you then, evil (sinful by nature) as you are, know how to give good and advantageous gifts to your children, how much more will your Father who is in heaven [perfect as He is] give what is good and advantageous to those who keep on asking Him.*

CHAPTER 15

AVOIDING THE DARK SIDE

T he seer dimensions are rife with deception. Some believe you cannot go wrong if you love Jesus, but that defies the Word of God. Jesus and the apostles consistently warned us about deception, error, strong delusions, and the like in the pages of Scripture. You can't read a book in the New Testament without a warning to believers about the work of the enemy.

Consider John the Beloved's warning in 1 John 4:1: *"Beloved, do not believe every spirit, but test the spirits, whether they are of God."* Paul warned us, *"There are, it may be, so many kinds of languages in the world, and none of them is without significance"* (1 Cor. 14:10). We know satan disguises himself as an angel of light (see 2 Cor. 11:14). And the heart is deceitful above all things (see Jer. 17:9).

Yes, false encounters, dreams, and visions can deceive seers—and seers can enter into spiritual dimensions illegally. You are seated in heavenly places in Christ and He is your legal entry point to everything in the spirit realm. Jesus is not only the door to salvation, He's also the door to the spirit realm. The Holy Spirit is your guide. Deceiving spirts—spirits that seek to kill, steal, and destroy your gift—lead you into seer dimensions through back doors, demonic portals, and loopholes in the spirit.

Remember the Holy Spirit is the Spirit of Truth (see John 16:13). Satan is the father of lies (see John 8:44). In these last days, we are seeing God pour out His Spirit with greater glory, but we are also seeing greater darkness (see Isa. 60:2). Anyone can be deceived. Let's look at some of the ways the enemy works deception in the seer dimension.

Vain Imaginations

The sanctified imagination is part of the seer dimension, but the enemy seeks to pervert our sight with vain imaginations. Often, unresolved hurts and wounds open the door for the enemy to convince us that what we see is from the Lord when it's really demonic. Rejection, bitterness, envy, and other toxic emotions can open us up to trusting in vain imaginations rather than casting them down. Vain imaginations build strongholds of deception in our souls that corrupt the seer gift. Paul wrote:

> *For the weapons of our warfare are not carnal but mighty in God for pulling down strongholds, casting down arguments and every high thing that exalts itself against the knowledge of God, bringing every thought into captivity to the obedience of Christ, and being ready to punish all disobedience when your obedience is fulfilled* (2 Corinthians 10:4-6).

Let the words discern the thoughts and intentions of your heart and cast down vain imaginations to avoid this snare.

Boasting and Exaggeration

Boasting and exaggeration are rooted in pride. When seers begin to boast in their gift instead of the gift giver or exaggerate what they see in the spirit to impress people, they are on a slippery slope that leads to deception.

There are many warnings in the Bible that seers and seeing people should heed. James warns that boasting in your arrogance is evil (see James 4:16). Jeremiah admonishes that the wise man should not boast in his wisdom (see Jer. 9:34). Solomon straightforwardly said to let someone else praise you instead of praising yourself (see Prov. 27:2).

Before Saul was Paul, he boasted in his spiritual lineage. Later, He boasted in his weakness (see 2 Cor. 11:30). He understood when he was weak, God was strong in his life and God's grace was perfected in his weakness (see 2 Cor. 12:9-11). Ask God for the grace of humility to avoid this trap.

A Biased Eye

If your eye is biased, you may see what other people want you to see rather than what God wants you to see. A bias is a bent or a tendency to favor one thing over another. It could be a prejudice but it could also just be a preference. Samuel was a seer and he had a bias. We see it manifest in 1 Samuel 16:1-7:

> *Now the Lord said to Samuel, "How long will you mourn for Saul, seeing I have rejected him from reigning over Israel? Fill your horn with oil, and go; I am sending you to Jesse the Bethlehemite. For I have provided Myself a king among his sons." And Samuel said, "How can I go? If Saul hears it, he will kill me."*
>
> *But the Lord said, "Take a heifer with you, and say, "I have come to sacrifice to the Lord." Then invite Jesse to the sacrifice, and I will show you what you shall do; you shall anoint for Me the one I name to you." So Samuel did what the Lord said, and went to Bethlehem. And the elders of*

the town trembled at his coming, and said, "Do you come peaceably?" And he said, "Peaceably; I have come to sacrifice to the Lord. Sanctify yourselves, and come with me to the sacrifice." Then he consecrated Jesse and his sons, and invited them to the sacrifice.

So it was, when they came, that he looked at Eliab and said, "Surely the Lord's anointed is before Him!" But the Lord said to Samuel, "Do not look at his appearance or at his physical stature, because I have refused him. For the Lord does not see as man sees; for man looks at the outward appearance, but the Lord looks at the heart."

Samuel was biased by tradition, because usually the first-born male would receive the greatest blessing. I believe he was also biased by the looks of Eliab. Samuel was a handsome, tall man and so was Eliab. Samuel did not immediately discern God's heart because of the bias. Ask the Lord to show you your own biases and remain aware of them so you can submit them to God.

Misguided Motives

Your motive in seer ministry should be to glorify God by edifying, comforting, exhorting, and warning God's people—and based on love. Anything else is misguided. If you are trying to impress people with your seeing, wring money out of people's pockets, make a name for yourself, or anything other than build God's agenda, you are polluting your prophetic flow.

Oftentimes when our motives are misguided, we don't know it because we're deceived. Proverbs 21:2 reveals, *"Every way of a man is right in his own eyes, but the Lord weighs the hearts."* And Proverbs 16:2 says, *"All the ways of a man are pure in his own eyes, but the Lord weighs the spirits."* Ask the Lord to purify your motives

Exalting Extrabiblical Revelation

Cults are born from extrabiblical revelation, but so also are minor errors that can turn into major blind spots. Although not everything you see is in the Bible, we are not called to establish new doctrines based on what we see in the spirit. Moreover, what we see in the spirit should line up with the precepts of the Word of God and the ways of God.

The Holy Spirit does not have vision problems. When we exalt extrabiblical revelations over the revelation of Christ, we're on dangerous ground. Ask the Lord to break any deception off your mind periodically to keep your mind free of darkness.

Presumption Sight

There are few things worse than a presumptuous seer. *Webster's Dictionary* defines *presume* as "to form an opinion from little or no evidence" and "to take as true or as a fact without actual proof." *Presumptuous* means to "overstep due bounds" and "take liberties." The Bible only mentions the words *presume, presumed, presumptuous*, and *presumptuously* 11 times, but it always carries a negative connotation.

Deuteronomy 18:20 says, *"But the prophet who presumes to speak a word in My name, which I have not commanded him to speak, or who speaks in the name of other gods, that prophet shall die."* We are living in a time of grace. But you can see that God hates presumption. Presumption can lead to false visions.

In Colossians 2:18-19, Paul warns, *"Do not let anyone cheat you of your reward by delighting in false humility and the worship of angels, dwelling on those things which he has not seen, vainly arrogant due to his unspiritual mind, and not supporting the head, from which the entire body, nourished and knit together by joints and sinews, grows as God gives the increase"* (MEV). Ask the Lord to help you avoid presumptuous sins to avoid this trap.

Self-Ambition and Self-Promotion

Anything "self" needs to be crucified. John the Baptist sought to decrease so Christ's ministry would increase (see John 3:30). We should seek to see Christ's ministry increase in our lives. We should seek to build Christ's kingdom. While marketing and promotion are necessary elements of getting the Word out about books and events, the spirit in which you promote yourself matters. There are boundaries to godly promotion.

Ambition in and of itself is not wrong. There are godly ambitions, but the line is thinner than some people realize. The self-ambitious seer wants to be noticed, wants to be promoted, wants to be applauded. James, the apostle of practical faith, asserted:

> But if you have bitter envy and self-seeking in your hearts, do not boast and lie against the truth. This wisdom does not descend from above, but is earthly, sensual, demonic. For where envy and self-seeking exist, confusion and every evil thing are there (James 3:14-16).

To avoid this trap, ask the Lord to root out of you any self-ambition and to warn you to curb the self-promotion before you cross the line.

Calculated Control and Manipulation

The Jezebel spirit—or just your flesh—will tempt you to use prophecy to control and manipulate people. As I said in my book *The Making of a Prophet*, prophetic people who flow in control and manipulation are welcoming the influence of Jezebel in their lives and ministries.

"Control and manipulation are tools the enemy uses to pervert prophetic ministry," I wrote. "To control someone is to exercise restraining or directing influence over, or to have power over him. Prophets need to exercise self-control through the power of the Holy Ghost, but have no business seeking to control anyone else. If you see traces of control and manipulation in your life, go on a crusade to rid yourself of these traits because they are earmarks of the Jezebel spirit."

To avoid this trap, ask the Lord to deliver you from the fear of man, which often drives control. Ask Him to deliver you from a desire for your will and your way and to help you submit to His will, His way, and His timing.

Pimping Out Your Gift

Second Peter 2:3 (KJV) tells us, *"And through covetousness shall they with feigned words make merchandise of you: whose judgment now of a long time lingereth not, and their damnation slumbereth not."* As you grow in the seer ministry and start gaining attention, the temptation will come to make merchandise of people—to exploit them—by using your gift for financial gain. This is one of the fastest ways to pervert your prophetic voice. Ask the Lord to help you avoid the love of money, which a root of all evil (see 1 Tim. 6:10), to avoid this deception.

Independent Spirit

First Corinthians 12:28 says: *"And God has appointed these in the church: first apostles, second prophets, third teachers, after that miracles, then gifts of healings, helps, administrations, varieties of tongues."* Where did God set prophets? In the church. True prophets understand that they shouldn't be free from the influence, guidance, and input from others. Why would you want to be? There is wisdom and protection in the counsel of many.

You won't go far and you won't last long in the seer ministry if you have a Rambo, got-to-do-it-my-way spirit. Prophets need to work with other ministry gifts and all need to be submitted to the King of Kings. Spiritual accountability is vital in this hour. We have to temper that though. Because blind obedience to a man can lead you into deception. Submit everything to the Word of God. Ask God to help you find the proper alignment and truly submit to godly counsel to avoid this deception.

Strange Fire

New Age practices have infiltrated the prophetic ministry. The Bible calls this *"strange fire"* (Lev. 10:1). The word *strange* in the passage means "unauthorized, foreign or profane." Prophetic operations that are not authorized by God—that are fabricated or pull from the flesh, the spirit of divination, or some other source—are strange fire. Avoid strange fire like the plague. It will kill your ministry fast. Ask the Lord to help you avoid the temptation to press past your gift and into an unauthorized dimension.

Back Doors in the Spirit

Many seers aren't satisfied with what the Lord shows them or some sort of offense or hurt will cause them to breach the legalities of the spirit. There are backdoors in the spirit through which seers can enter the spirit world illegally and use a God-given gift to look into people's lives. Seers can also knowingly or unknowingly work with or be deceived by familiar spirits to obtain information. Keep your heart free from offense and be content with what the Lord chooses to show you to avoid this deception.

A Prophetic Word About Deception

In my book *Victory Decrees*, I share prophetic words from the Holy Spirit about spiritual warfare. Let this entry edify and encourage you to search your heart. The Lord said, "If you were deceived would you know it? Of course, you would not know you were deceived because that is the very essence of deception. Do not be afraid, but do not presume you are not believing a lie. If you do not have peace, if you do not have joy, if you do not see breakthrough, if you are not walking in the fullness of your calling, you are believing some sort of lie. You may have learned this as a child or as an adult. It doesn't matter when the deception came. What matters is you break that deception and embrace the truth that keeps you free. Acknowledge the possibility of deception in your life and ask Me to break it off your mind."

Let this be your prayer and decree:

> *Father, break any and all deception off my mind and my heart. Help me discern the areas of my life where Your Word is not ruling and reigning in my soul. I decree the light of God is shining in my heart and roots out all forms of deception. I declare that deception cannot stand in my life because I am a lover of the truth.*

CONCLUSION
AND PRAYER

When you were born again, you regained the right to see in the spirit. Jesus said we cannot "see" the kingdom of God unless we are born again (see John 3:5). When you accepted Jesus as Lord and Savior, Satan's blinders were legally removed and your spiritual eyes became new. In other words, when old things passed away and all things became new according to 2 Corinthians 5:17, your spiritual eyes were restored.

I join my faith with Paul's prayer in Ephesians 1 and declare that God is opening the eyes of your heart and giving you wisdom, knowledge, and revelation even now. Just as the scales fell off Saul's eyes in the Book of Acts as he encountered the risen Christ, I pray any remaining scales, blinders, and filters the enemy has put over your eyes fall as you agree with this prayer. I decree you can see. I pray:

> *Father, please give my readers the Spirit of wisdom and revelation in the knowledge of You, that the eyes of their understanding may be enlightened, that they may know what*

is the hope of Your calling and what are the riches of the glory of Your inheritance among the saints, and what is the surpassing greatness of Your power toward them who believe, according to the working of Your mighty power, which You performed in Christ when You raised Him from the dead and seated Him at Your own right hand in the heavenly places, far above all principalities, and power, and might, and dominion, and every name that is named, not only in this age but also in that which is to come.

I release impartation and activation to their eyes to enter the seer dimension according to the will of God. I ask You, Father, to fill them again with Your Holy Spirit so that they may walk worthy of Your calling.

I impart and activate dreams and the gift of interpretation of dreams, in Jesus' name. I release an impartation for visual revelation and the wisdom to judge what is seen in the spirit, in Jesus' name.

I ask You, Father, to pull back the veil on the angelic dimension so we can see angels, receive messages from angels, and otherwise interact with the heavenly host according to Your divine purposes, in Jesus' name.

I ask You, Father, to open the heavens and allow us see into the throne room, to encounter Your Spirit in the heavenly dimension, and to experience a taste of heaven in this life, in Jesus' name. I ask You, Father, to allow us to see into the demonic dimension for purposes of destroying the works of darkness, in Jesus' name.

I ask You, Father, to usher us into the ecstatic realm so we can experience trances, out-of-body experiences, spirit travel, deep sleep, and other supernatural encounters that help us to accomplish Your will in the earth and to know You more, in Jesus' name.

Help us, Lord, to prepare ourselves to enter the secret dimension and ready ourselves to enter the silent dimension. Help us, God, to set ourselves apart to meditate on Your Word, Your emotions, Your character, Your ways, and Your promises, in Jesus' name. Amen.

NOTES

Chapter 1 Calling All Seers

1. *Merriam-Webster* s.v. "seer," accessed May 25, 2019, https://www
   .merriam-webster.com/dictionary/seer.
2. William D. Mounce, *Mounce's Complete Expository Dictionary of Old and
   New Testament Words* (Grand Rapids, MI: Zondervan Academic, 2009).
3. Mounce, *Mounce's Complete Expository Dictionary of Old and New
   Testament Words*.
4. Bible Hub, s.v. "*ro'eh*," accessed May 25, 2019, https://biblehub.com/
   hebrew/7203.htm.
5. John Paul Jackson, "Prophets & Seers" Identify Network Inc., accessed
   May 25, 2019, https://www.identitynetwork.net/apps/articles/default.asp
   ?articleid=15737&columnid=2093.
6. Jackson, "Prophets & Seers."
7. Jennifer LeClaire, "When a Vision of Raising the Dead Becomes
   Reality," Charisma Media, accessed May 25, 2019, https://www
   .charismamag.com/blogs/the-plumb-line/24319-when-a-vision-of-raising
   -the-dead-becomes-reality.
8. Ibid.
9. Ibid.
10. Ibid.
11. Ibid.
12. Ibid.
13. Ibid.
14. Ibid.
15. Jeff Jansen, "Paul Cain's Passing Message to Us—as a Sign from Heaven,"
    OpenHeaven.com, February 15, 2019, https://www .openheaven
    .com/forums/topic/paul-cains-passing-message-to-us-as-a-sign-from
    -heaven-by-jeff-jansen/.

16. "Paul Cain StadiumChristianityProphecy," YouTube, 2:14, May 2, 2016, https://www.youtube.com/watch?v=nCVSXNsodk0.

17. Bob Jones, "What Is a Seer," Divine Council, accessed May 25, 2019, https://divinecouncil.org/forum/threads/what-is-a-seer-by-bob-jones.527/.

18. Jones, "What Is a Seer."

19. ADR Investments LLC, "Last Night While You Were Dreaming, You Got Mail! John Paul Jackson Explores Power of Dreams and Mysteries In New Show," press release, October 2, 2013, http://lightningreleases .com/last-night-while-you-were-dreaming-you-got-mail-john-paul-jackson -explores-power-of-dreams-and-mysteries-in-new-show/.

20. "Trump Prophecies Connected to Election and the Year 2017 House of Destiny, April 20, 2013, https://www.houseofdestiny.org/trump -prophecies-connected-to-election-and-the-year-2017/.

21. "Kim Clement Prophesied About May 18th 2018," YouTube, 1:10, https:// www.youtube.com/watch?v=UYVIRgQQcOs.

22. Jim W. Goll, *The Seer* (Shippensburg, PA: Destiny Image Publishers Inc., 2004), 47.

Chapter 2 Everyone Can See in the Spirit

1. Bible Study Tools, s.v. "*zeloo*," accessed May 27, 2019, https://www .biblestudytools.com/lexicons/greek/kjv/zeloo.html.

Chapter 3 Three Dimensions of Man

1. Kenneth E. Hagin, *The Human Spirit Volume 2: Of the Spirit, Soul, and Body Series* (Tulsa, OK: Kenneth Hagin Ministries, 1994), https:// issacharpropheticcity.files.wordpress.com/2015/01/the-human-spirit-by -kenneth-hagin.pdf.

Chapter 4 The Dream Dimension

1. "How Often Do We Dream?" National Sleep Foundation, accessed May 29, 2019, https://www.sleep.org/articles/how-often-dreams/.

Chapter 5 The Vision Dimension

1. Bible Hub, s.v. "*chazah*," accessed May 29, 2019, https://biblehub.com/ hebrew/2377.htm.

2. Bible Hub, s.v. "*horasis,*" accessed May 29, 2019, https://biblehub.com/ greek/3706.htm.

Chapter 6 The Angelic Dimension

1. Bible Study Tools, s.v. "*lanthano,*" accessed May 29, 2019, https://www
.biblestudytools.com/lexicons/greek/kjv/lanthano.html.
2. Dutch Sheets, "Mercy Is Our New Currency," Dutch Sheets Ministries,
December 13, 2016, http://dutchsheets.mybigcommerce.com/blog/
mercy-is-our-new-currency/.
3. "Angelic Visitation, Vision, Healing," Bethel, July 12, 2011, http://www
.ibethel.org/testimonies/angelic-visitation-vision-healing/.
4. Tim Sheets, *Angel Armies* (Shippensburg, PA: Destiny Image Publishers
Inc., 2016), 26–27.
5. Bible Hub, s.v. "Machanayim," accessed May 30, 2019, https://biblehub
.com/hebrew/4266.htm.
6. Sheets, *Angel Armies,* 28–29.
7. "NASA Armstrong Fact Sheet: Sonic Booms," National Aeronautics and
Space Administration, updated August 15, 2017, https://www.nasa.gov/
centers/armstrong/news/FactSheets/FS-016-DFRC.html.

Chapter 7 The Heavenly Dimension

1. Charles Ferguson Ball, *Heaven* (Wheaton, IL: Victor Books, 1980).
2. "Americans Love God and the Bible, Are Fuzzy on the Details," LifeWay
Research, September 27, 2016, https://lifewayresearch.com/2016/09/27/
americans-love-god-and-the-bible-are-fuzzy-on-the-details/.
3. Bob Jones with Sandy Warner, "'Did You Learn to Love?'—Bob Jones'
Testimony From His August 8, 1976 Death Experience," Elijah List,
February 18, 2014, http://www.elijahlist.com/words/display_word
.html?ID=13128.
4. *Merriam-Webster,* s.v. "imagination," accessed May 29, 2019, https://www
.merriam-webster.com/dictionary/imagination.

Chapter 8 The Demonic Dimension

1. Laurie Ditto, *The Hell Conspiracy* (Shippensburg, PA: Destiny Image
Publishers Inc., 2019).
2. Laurie Ditto, "Transported to Hell: The Things I Saw Changed
Me Forever!," Destiny Image, accessed May 31, 2019, https://www
.destinyimage.com/2019/04/15/the-things-i-saw-in-hell/.

Chapter 9 The Ecstatic Dimension

1. *Merriam-Webster,* s.v. "mystical," accessed May 31, 2019, https://www
.merriam-webster.com/dictionary/mystical.

2. Bible Study Tools, s.v. "*musterion*," accessed May 31, 2019, https://www
   .biblestudytools.com/lexicons/greek/kjv/musterion.html.

3. W. E. Vine, *W. E. Vine's New Testament Word Pictures: Romans to
   Revelation,* (Nashville: Thomas Nelson, 2015), 567.

4. William Johnston ed., *The Cloud of Unknowing and The Book of Privy
   Counseling* (New York: Image, 1973). https://www.amazon.com/
   Cloud-Unknowing-Book-Privy-Counseling/dp/0385030975.

Chapter 10 The Trance Dimension

1. *Webster's Dictionary 1828* - Online Edition, s.v. "trance," accessed May 31,
   2019, http://webstersdictionary1828.com/Dictionary/trance.

2. Bible Study Tools, s.v. "trance," accessed May 30, 2019, https://www
   .biblestudytools.com/dictionary/trance/.

3. Bible Study Tools, s.v. "*ekstasis*," accessed May 30, 2019, https://
   www .biblestudytools.com/commentaries/revelation/revelation-1/
   revelation-1-10.html.

4. *Smith's Bible Dictionary,* s.v. "trance," Christianity.com, accessed
   May 31, 2019, https://www.christianity.com/bible/dictionary.php
   ?dict=sbd&id=4355.

5. Bible Study Tools, s.v. "trance," accessed May 31, 2019, https://www
   .biblestudytools.com/encyclopedias/isbe/trance.html.

6. Jennifer LeClaire, "Is 'Trance Evangelism' Coming Back In Vogue?"
   Charisma Media, accessed May 31, 2019, https://www.charismamag.com/
   blogs/the-plumb-line/24037-is-trance-evangelism-coming-back-in-vogue.

Chapter 11 The Out-of-Body Dimension

1. Kenneth E. Hagin, *The Art of Intercession* (Tulsa, OK: RHEMA Bible
   Church, 1980), 131–132.

2. Matthew Poole, *A Commentary on the Holy Bible* (London: Banner of
   Truth Trust, 1969), 412.

3. Bible Study Tools, s.v. "Acts 8:39," accessed June 2, 2019, https://www
   .biblestudytools.com/commentaries/gills-exposition-of-the-bible/acts-8-39.
   html.

4. Sid Roth, *It's Supernatural!,* "Patricia King," February 1, 2010, https://
   sidroth.org/television/tv-archives/patricia-king/.

Chapter 13 The Silent Dimension

1. Mirabai Starr, *Saint John of the Cross: Devotions, Prayers and Living
   Wisdom* (Boulder, CO: Sounds True, Inc., 2012), 47.

2. Edith Stein, *The Silence of the Cross: The Collected Works of Edit Stein* (Washington, DC:ICS Publications, 2003), 83.

3. BJ Gonzalvo, *Lessons in Leadership from the Saints: Called to Holiness, Called to Lead* (Bloomington, IN: WestBowPress, 2017).

4. Mike Bickle, "Contemplative Prayer," transcript, July 20, 2001, https:// ihopkcorg-a.akamaihd.net/platform/IHOP/979/82/20010720-T -Introductory_Principles_to_Contemplative_Prayer_Part_1_CTP02.pdf.

5. Focus on the Family, "Questions and Concerns About Contemplative Prayer," accessed August 24, 2019, https://www.focusonthefamily.com/ family-qa/questions-and-concerns-about-contemplative-prayer.

6. James Goll, "Why We Need This Ancient Christian Practice Now More Than Ever," Charisma Media, February 24, 2019, https:// ministrytodaymag.com/life/prayer/25859-why-we-need-this-ancient -christian-practice-now-more-than-ever.

7. Saint John of the Cross, *The Collected Works of Saint John of the Cross,* translated by Kieran Kavanaugh and Otilio Rodriguez (Washington, DC: Institute of Carmelite Studies, 1991), 382.

8. Christoph von Schönborn and Michael J. Miller, *The Joy of Being a Priest: Following the Curé of Ars* (San Francisco, CA: Ignatius Press, 2010), 89.

9. Ray Simpson, *Exploring Celtic Spirituality* (London: Hodder & Stoughton, 1995).

10. David Bentley Hart, *The Experience of God* (London: Yale University Press, 2013), 321.

11. J. Brent Bill, *Holy Silence: The Gift of Quaker Spirituality* (Brewster, MA: Paraclete Press, 2005), 7.

12. James Goll, qtd. in Craig von Buseck, "What is Soaking Prayer?" CBN .com, https://www1.cbn.com/question/what-is-soaking-prayer.

13. Dick Eastman, *The Hour That Changes the World: A Practical Plan for Personal Prayer* (Grand Rapids, MI: Chosen Books, 2002), 41.

Chapter 14 Meditation: A Master Key to Mystical Dimensions

1. St. Teresa of Avila, *The Interior Castle* (New York, NY: Dover Thrift Editions, 2008), 18.

2. Bible Study Tools, s.v. "*hagah*," accessed June 2, 2019, https://www .biblestudytools.com/lexicons/hebrew/nas/hagah.html.

3. Barbie Breathitt, *Gateway to the Seer Realm* (Shippensburg, PA: Destiny Image Publishers Inc., 2012).

ABOUT
JENNIFER LECLAIRE

Jennifer is senior leader of Awakening House of Prayer in Fort Lauderdale, FL, founder of the Ignite Network, and founder of the Awakening Blaze prayer movement. Jennifer formerly served as the first-ever female editor of *Charisma* magazine and is a prolific author of over 25 books.

You can find Jennifer online or shoot her an email at info@jenniferleclaire.org.

Made in the USA
Columbia, SC
02 August 2024

39858321R00098